THE DOVE'S NEST

RESTAURANT

From our nest to yours,

Cindy Burch

THE DOVE'S NEST
RESTAURANT

NEW AMERICAN RECIPES FROM A HISTORIC TEXAS TOWN

By Cindy Burch
Illustrated by Marilyn Goss Harris

To order additional cookbooks, other products, or to make reservations:

Call (972) 938-DOVE (3683) or write us at:
The Dove's Nest
105 West Jefferson Street
Waxahachie, Texas 75165
FAX: (972) 938-7974

If you plan to visit, we are located thirty miles south of Dallas, Texas (between Dallas and Waco), on
Interstate 35. Take exit 287 Business and go one mile to the Waxahachie Town Square.

Published by The Dove's Nest

Copyright: The Dove's Nest
105 West Jefferson Street
Waxahachie, Texas 75165

Library of Congress Number: 96-86128
ISBN: 0-9653257-0-9

Edited, Designed, and Manufactured by
Favorite Recipes® Press
P.O. Box 305142
Nashville, Tennessee 37230
1-(800)-358-0560
Managing Editor: Mary Cummings
Project Manager: Debbie Van Mol
Cover Art and Illustrations: Marilyn Goss Harris
Cover Photography: Jim Shows
Book Design: Starletta Polster
Typographer: Sara Anglin

Manufactured in the United States
First Printing: 1996   7,500 copies
Second Printing: 1997   7,500 copies
Third Printing: 2002   5,000 copies

Dedication

To my parents, Marilyn and Tiny Goss, whose love, support and a lifetime of encouragement have always given me courage to do what I believe in. My Dad passed away in 1998, but I will always be grateful to him, and my Mom, for laying a Christian foundation upon which they raised me and taught me I can do all things through Christ who strengthens me.

My Parents

A Note from Cindy . . .

I have found that some of life's warmest moments occur around the dinner table when we're sharing good food and conversation with family and friends. As far back as I can remember, food was always the guest of honor at family gatherings. Both of my grandmothers, one from Alabama and the other from Texas, were true southern cooks and taught me the first lessons in "culinary art"— southern style. I can hardly remember a time that they weren't standing over a stove cooking something scrumptious. They would no sooner have breakfast made than they would get started on lunch, often baking a couple of pies in between.

My grandmother on my dad's side we called "Big Mama." She raised four boys with a spatula in one hand and a belt in the other. The youngest of the four is my dad, whom she called her "baby," even though he was the largest defensive tackle in the Southwest Conference and went on to play pro football with the Cleveland Browns and the New York Giants. Big Mama loved to have her boys home with their families for chicken-fried steak, butter beans and cornbread, mashed potatoes with cream gravy, and sweetened ice tea. Although she passed away in 1976, we all still crave her chicken and dumplings.

My other grandmother we called "Nanny." She lived in Tuscaloosa, Alabama, where my mom grew up with her sister and two brothers. Nanny wasn't happy either if she didn't have a house full of mouths to feed, including the preacher who came for Sunday dinner. I remember she always had wonderful home-canned vegetables from her garden, and she won baking contests with her homemade candy and desserts.

The other influential cook in my life is my mom, who bought me my first children's kitchen set and allowed me to be her "little helper" as she prepared dinner or baked a batch of her famous oatmeal cookies. My parents entertained a lot and they took me, an only child, to many wonderful restaurants and events that exposed me at an early age to fine cuisine and the art of catering. As I became older, Mom let me have full run of the kitchen and as I read cookbooks from cover to cover, I began

teaching myself other types of cuisine—mainly the New American approach from which I not only drew on my southern heritage, but integrated other tastes from around the world. My mom is also an acclaimed artist, well known in the Southwest for her paintings of children in school, at play, and on Christmas cards. She doesn't name her work, but each one contains a hidden scripture verse and one or several white doves, because in 1968 a white dove flew into an open window of her art class when she was teaching in a Dallas elementary school. It was a time when the values we held dear were removed from the classrooms of America and she was looking for a sign of encouragement as to what direction her career was to take. She trusted in God and resigned a fourteen-year teaching career and began anew as a professional artist, author, and speaker.

In 1986, Mom opened a gift shop and art gallery on the historic town square of Waxahachie, Texas, where I helped her publish her first children's book and launch her products on the national market.

It wasn't until I married Andrew Burch in 1992 that my love for cooking found its way to becoming a business. Andrew also came from a family of great cooks and was working in the food service business when we married. Together we opened a little restaurant in the back of my mom's gift shop and called ourselves Marilyn's Art & Tearoom. We had a tiny kitchen with household appliances, and quietly began preparing lunch each day for hungry tourists and the people of Ellis County. To our delight, we found our thirty-seat tearoom filled with customers who loved our food, and many more waiting to be seated.

Within months, Andrew quit his full-time job to take over the business end of things, while I prepared as much food as I could every morning, along with a sweet little lady who would tirelessly appear each day to bake homemade pies, cakes, and cobblers. We wondered at times if we had taken on too much of a task, but every month got easier and the joy we seemed to bring to our satisfied customers made it all worthwhile.

We had more than outgrown our tiny space when an opportunity came to buy the original old hardware store in Waxahachie that was built in 1913 by the Moore family. This was a major step for a young married couple who hadn't yet bought their first home. But with the Lord's will we stepped out in faith and our tiny tearoom has now become a beautiful restaurant—serving over one hundred hungry mouths daily. Our precious Lord has continued to bless us each day and we are constantly reminded of His promise that He will supply all our needs according to His riches in Heaven.

Together we have tried to include the cornerstones of our kitchen in this cookbook with favorite recipes from both our lunch and dinner menu. We hope that you will be able to feel a little of the pleasure that we have had cooking for you, and, in turn, that you will prepare our recipes to bring pleasure to your friends and family as well.

Cindy Burch

TABLE OF CONTENTS

Ellis County Courthouse

Ellis County Courthouse

Waxahachie, Texas

Waxahachie, Texas, home of The Dove's Nest, is recognized today for its invigorating ambiance, simple beauty, and comfortable lifestyle. A colony established in the mid-1800s, Waxahachie was settled by cotton barons who had made their fortunes during the King Cotton era. The town is best known for its splendid gingerbread-trimmed homes and its magnificent courthouse that sits on the town square, just up the street from The Dove's Nest.

The Ellis County Courthouse was built in 1895. Author James Michener described it as "a fairy tale palace . . . one of the finest buildings in Texas." An Italian sculptor named Harry Hurley was invited to Waxahachie to create in the huge stacks of red sandstone the intricate carvings that enhance the beautiful courthouse.

Hurley lived in a boarding house in Waxahachie during the many months that it took him to carve the huge blocks by hand. The woman who ran the boarding house had a daughter, named Mable Frame, whose classic features fired the imagination of the guest sculptor so much that he carved her face into the handsome exterior of the courthouse arches. As legend has it, although Hurley had fallen in love with Mable, she was not in love with him. The heartbroken Hurley apparently didn't handle rejection well, and out of spite began carving faces with a vengeance. Mouths were turned into frowns and smiles were made into toothless grins. Some of the faces even resemble demons and gargoyles.

By the time the cotton-rich farmers and cattlemen who had hired Hurley realized what he was doing, it was too late. Waxahachie townspeople then ran him out of town and no one seems to know what happened to the rejected artist.

Thank You's . . .

This book is hardly the work of a single person, despite the credit on the cover. The know-how of a lot of people is bound between these covers, and if it weren't for them, it would never have gotten done. So with a grateful heart, I would like to thank—

Our wonderful and loyal customers and friends who love our food and who encouraged me to write this book and include their favorite recipes.

Andrew Burch, my partner in life and business, who takes leaps of faith with me everyday in the world of running a restaurant. I love you and could not do it without your help.

Marilyn Goss Harris, my precious mom, for taking time out of her busy schedule to illustrate my first cookbook and make it extra special.

Martha Stewart, whose autographed copy of *Entertaining* I received from my mom on Christmas morning in 1982. She inspired me to begin the journey not only of preparing good food, but in presenting it in a beautiful way.

Our kitchen and wait staff—for without their hard work we could not serve our many hungry customers each day.

Sandra Walker and Denise Riley, who so diligently manage our Jefferson Street Antique Mall and our gift shop, Marilyn's Art Room. I could never do all the tasks the restaurant requires without these two angels overlooking the rest of the building.

Carolyn, Paul, and Judson Burch, my in-laws, who not only give us much love and encouragement, but prepare us great Sunday night dinners after a long week running the restaurant. They even double as wait staff, cashiers, and dishwashers when we get in a real bind.

Dave Kempf, Debbie Van Mol, Mary Cummings, Steve Newman and all the folks at Favorite Recipes® Press, who are without a doubt some of the nicest people I've ever had the pleasure to work with. Thank you for making this book a reality.

And finally . . . our girls, "Abby," "Cinnamon," and "Classy," who gave their paws of approval as they walked over all my pages and recipes while working on this book.

Beginnings

Beginnings

Almond Bacon Cheddar Spread, 15

Caviar Pie, 16

Curried Crab in Endive Spears, 17

Goat Cheese and Pesto Torta, 18

Mustard Ginger Shrimp Canapés, 19

Hot Artichoke Dip, 20

Roasted Red Pepper Dip, 21

Chicken Apricot Chile Relleno with Black Bean Sauce and
Smoked Tomato Curry Sauce, 22

Parmesan Chicken Tenders, 25

Crab Cakes on Cornmeal Biscuits with Tartar Sauce, 26

Curried Cheese and Chutney Turnovers, 29

Duck Ravioli with Apple Cider Cream Sauce, 30

Marinated Meatballs, 32

Pecan Cornmeal Breaded Oysters with Smoked Shallot Remoulade Sauce, 33

Sausage and Sage Hand Pies, 34

Andrew's Eggnog, 35

Orange Spiced Iced Tea, 35

Strawberry Lemonade, 36

Almond Bacon Cheddar Spread

yields 3 cups

*This spread makes a delicious sandwich on toasted bread. I served it as part of
a sandwich medley when I first opened the tea room. Serve it within a few hours—it doesn't keep.
But it sure is good for a few hours—if it lasts that long.*

12 strips bacon, crisp-fried, crumbled
2 cups shredded Cheddar cheese
$^{1}/_{2}$ cup chopped toasted almonds
$^{1}/_{4}$ cup chopped green onions
$^{1}/_{2}$ cup mayonnaise
Dash of Tabasco sauce

Combine the bacon, cheese, almonds, green onions, mayonnaise and Tabasco sauce in a medium bowl; mix well.

Serve as a spread with crackers and fresh fruit or as a filling for sandwiches.

Caviar Pie

yields 8 to 12 servings

This is very popular even with people who think they don't like caviar.
I use red (salmon) caviar for Christmas parties.

8 ounces cream cheese, softened
1/4 cup mayonnaise
1 tablespoon minced onion
2 teaspoons Worcestershire sauce
2 teaspoons fresh lemon juice
Caviar
6 hard-cooked eggs, grated
1/4 cup finely chopped onion
Small toast rounds

Cream the cream cheese and the mayonnaise in a mixer bowl until light and fluffy. Season with the minced onion, Worcestershire sauce and lemon juice.

Spread in a 1-inch thick circle in the center of a serving plate. Cover the surface with caviar.

Sprinkle with the grated eggs and chopped onion.

Chill until serving time.

Serve with toast rounds.

Curried Crab in Endive Spears

yields 24 servings

Endive spears make an impressive presentation when arranged end to end on a platter.
At Christmas time, arrange fresh cranberries down the center of the tray.

1/4 cup mayonnaise
2 tablespoons minced celery
2 tablespoons minced onion
1 teaspoon curry powder
1 cup crab meat
Salt and freshly ground pepper to taste
4 heads Belgian endive, spears separated
Fresh alfalfa sprouts

Combine the mayonnaise, celery, onion and curry powder in a bowl; mix well.

Stir in the crab meat. Add salt and pepper; mix well.

Place 1 heaping teaspoon of the mixture at the base of each endive spear and place on a serving tray. Top with alfalfa sprouts.

The crab meat mixture may be prepared up to 8 hours in advance and chilled until ready to serve.

Goat Cheese and Pesto Torta

yields 24 servings

Layers of goat cheese and pesto make a dramatic presentation for a party centerpiece.

16 ounces cream cheese, softened
8 ounces goat cheese, softened
4 ounces prepared basil pesto
4 ounces prepared sun-dried tomato pesto
1/4 cup pine nuts, toasted
1 sprig of fresh basil

❧ Line a 6-inch flowerpot or an 8-cup mold with a piece of dry cheesecloth. Smooth out the surface and drape the excess over the side.

❧ Cream the cream cheese and goat cheese in a mixer bowl until light and fluffy. Reserve a small amount of the cheese mixture.

❧ Layer the remaining cheese mixture, basil pesto, cheese mixture and tomato pesto alternately in the prepared flowerpot until all the ingredients are used. Top with the reserved cheese mixture.

❧ Fold the excess cheesecloth over the top, pressing firmly. Chill for 2 hours.

❧ Invert onto a serving dish; remove the cheesecloth gently.

❧ Arrange the pine nuts in a circle on top of the cheese layer. Garnish with a sprig of basil in the center.

❧ Serve with crackers or fresh vegetables.

Mustard Ginger Shrimp Canapés

yields 50 servings

1 cup cider vinegar
3/4 cup vegetable oil
2 tablespoons sugar
1 tablespoon Worcestershire sauce
1 teaspoon Tabasco sauce
2 teaspoons dry mustard
4 1/2 teaspoons minced peeled gingerroot
Salt and black pepper to taste
2 pounds medium shrimp, peeled (about 50)
1 cup julienne strips of red, yellow and green bell peppers
Pita bread
1/4 cup finely chopped fresh cilantro
Hot red pepper flakes to taste
Sprigs of cilantro

Combine the vinegar, oil, sugar, Worcestershire sauce, Tabasco sauce, mustard, gingerroot, salt and black pepper in a saucepan; whisk briskly.

Bring to a boil; reduce heat. Simmer for 5 minutes, stirring occasionally.

Add the shrimp. Simmer for 3 to 5 minutes or until the shrimp are cooked through, stirring occasionally.

Transfer the mixture to a heatproof bowl. Stir in the bell peppers. Chill, covered, for 2 hours.

Cut each whole pita bread into 6 wedges. Toast lightly.

Drain and discard the liquid from the shrimp mixture. Stir in the cilantro, red pepper flakes, salt and black pepper.

Arrange a shrimp and several pepper strips on each pita wedge.

Garnish with sprigs of cilantro.

Hot Artichoke Dip

yields 24 servings

A delicious dip and very popular at our catered events.

28 ounces artichoke hearts, drained
1 cup sour cream
1/4 cup cream cheese, softened
4 ounces goat cheese
1/2 cup chopped green onions
1 teaspoon salt
1 tablespoon lemon juice
1/2 cup grated Parmesan cheese

Place the artichokes in a food processor container.

Process until coarsely chopped.

Combine the artichokes, sour cream, cream cheese, goat cheese, green onions, salt and lemon juice in a bowl; mix well.

Transfer to a baking dish. Sprinkle with the Parmesan cheese.

Bake at 350 degrees for 30 minutes.

Serve warm in a chafing dish or at room temperature with crackers.

Roasted Red Pepper Dip

yields 3 cups

I serve this dip in hollowed-out cabbages or peppers, nestled in an array of crudités.

4 roasted red bell peppers, chopped (page 140)
2 tablespoons sugar
16 ounces cream cheese, softened
Juice of 1 lemon
1 teaspoon salt

Purée the bell peppers in a blender. Strain through a fine sieve.

Place the mixture in a medium saucepan. Cook over medium or low heat until the mixture is reduced to a paste.

Mix with the sugar, cream cheese, lemon juice and salt in a bowl, beating until smooth; adjust seasonings to taste.

Serve with assorted crudités.

Chicken Apricot Chile Relleno with Black Bean Sauce and Smoked Tomato Curry Sauce

yields 8 servings

When The Dove's Nest received a three-and-one-half-star rating in The Dallas Morning News in August 1995, this was one of the dishes food columnist, Waltrina Stovall, reviewed as a stand out.

8 whole roasted Anaheim, California or Poblano chiles (page 140)
2 cups The Dove's Nest Chicken Apricot Salad (page 65)
2 cups flour
Salt to taste
8 eggs, beaten
2 cups cornmeal
1/4 cup vegetable oil
Black Bean Sauce (page 23)
Smoked Tomato Curry Sauce (page 24)

Remove only the tops and seeds from the chiles.

Stuff the chiles with the Chicken Apricot Salad using a spoon or pastry bag with no tip.

Dust with a mixture of the flour and salt. Dip in the eggs. Coat with a mixture of cornmeal and salt.

Sauté in hot oil in a skillet until golden brown.

Place the cooked chiles on a serving plate. Spoon the Black Bean Sauce and the Smoked Tomato Curry Sauce over and around the chiles.

Black Bean Sauce

yields 8 servings

1 cup dried black beans
6 cups water
3 strips bacon
1 cup chopped onion
2 tablespoons minced garlic
1 tablespoon each chili powder and cumin
3 cups chicken stock
1 bunch cilantro
Juice of 4 limes
Salt to taste

🌿 Sort and rinse the beans. Soak the beans in a large pan with the water overnight; drain.

🌿 Sauté the bacon, onion and garlic in a large saucepan for 5 minutes or until the onion is translucent.

🌿 Add the chili powder and cumin. Cook for 1 minute longer.

🌿 Add the beans and chicken stock. Simmer for 1 hour.

🌿 Pour the mixture into a food processor. Process until puréed.

🌿 Stir in the cilantro, lime juice and salt.

Smoked Tomato Curry Sauce

yields 8 servings

10 Roma tomatoes, cut into halves
3 cloves of garlic
1 small onion, cut into halves
2 tablespoons vegetable oil
1 tablespoon curry powder
1/2 cup white wine
Salt to taste
Juice of 1 lemon

Smoke the tomatoes, garlic and onion. (See page 141 for instructions on Smoking.)

Sauté in the oil in a skillet for 5 minutes. Add the curry powder.

Cook for 1 minute longer. Add the wine.

Cook for 5 minutes longer.

Purée the mixture and strain into a saucepan.

Simmer until reduced to the desired consistency.

Remove from heat and season with the salt and lemon juice.

Parmesan Chicken Tenders

yields 24 servings

Brant taught me this recipe for large receptions. Guests love them.

4 pounds chicken tenders
2^1/$_2$ cups butter
6 cups grated Romano or Parmesan cheese
1 cup whipping cream

Rinse the chicken and pat dry.

Combine 2 cups of the butter with the cheese and whipping cream in a heavy skillet.

Heat over low heat until the butter is melted, stirring frequently. Remove from heat and cover to keep warm.

Sauté the chicken in the remaining ^{1}/$_2$ cup butter in a skillet until cooked through and browned.

Place the chicken in a chafing dish. Pour the sauce evenly over the chicken. Serve hot.

Crab Cakes on Cornmeal Biscuits with Tartar Sauce

yields 36 servings

8 ounces lump crab meat, flaked and drained, or canned crab meat
1¹/₂ cups fresh bread crumbs
1 scallion, finely chopped
1 tablespoon chopped Italian parsley
1 large egg, lightly beaten
¹/₄ cup mayonnaise
2 teaspoons Dijon mustard
2 teaspoons fresh lemon juice
¹/₄ teaspoon Worcestershire sauce
¹/₂ teaspoon kosher salt
Freshly ground black pepper to taste
Vegetable oil
Cornmeal Biscuits (page 27)
Tartar Sauce (page 28)

Combine the crab meat, bread crumbs, scallion, parsley, egg, mayonnaise, mustard, lemon juice, Worcestershire sauce, salt and pepper in a medium bowl; mix well.

Shape 2 teaspoons of the mixture at a time into thirty-six ³/₄-inch patties. The crab cakes may be refrigerated at this point for up to 6 hours.

Heat 2 inches of oil in a large heavy skillet over medium-high heat.

Brown the crab cakes in the hot oil on one side for 1 minute. Turn and brown for 45 seconds. Drain on paper towels.

Split the Cornmeal Biscuits into halves horizontally. Place a crab cake on the bottom half of each biscuit.

Top with a generous amount of Tartar Sauce and replace the top of each biscuit.

Cornmeal Biscuits

yields 36 servings

4 medium jalapeños, seeded and cut into fourths
1³/4 cups plus 2 tablespoons flour
1¹/4 cups yellow cornmeal
4 teaspoons baking powder
1 tablespoon sugar
1¹/2 teaspoons kosher salt
1 large egg
1 cup milk
3 tablespoons vegetable oil

Combine the jalapeños, flour, cornmeal, baking powder, sugar and salt in a food processor container. Process until thoroughly mixed.

Add the egg, milk and oil. Process for 1 to 2 minutes until mixed.

Place the dough on a floured surface. Knead 2 to 3 times. Pat the dough into a ¹/2-inch thick circle. Cut with a 1¹/2-inch biscuit cutter, flouring the cutter frequently to prevent sticking.

Place the biscuits 1 inch apart on a baking sheet lined with parchment paper.

Place the baking sheet on rack in lower third of oven.

Bake at 350 degrees for 15 minutes. Remove to a wire rack to cool.

Tartar Sauce

yields 2¹/2 cups

2 cups mayonnaise
2 tablespoons white wine vinegar
3 sweet gherkins, minced
3 scallions, minced
¹/4 cup plus 2 tablespoons capers, drained

❧ Combine the mayonnaise, vinegar, gherkins, scallions and capers in a small bowl; mix well.

❧ Chill, covered, until serving time. The sauce will keep for up to 1 week in the refrigerator.

Curried Cheese and Chutney Turnovers

yields 32 servings

3 ounces light cream cheese, softened
1/2 cup packed shredded sharp white Cheddar cheese
1/3 cup finely chopped green onions
1 teaspoon curry powder
1/4 cup plus 2 1/2 teaspoons chopped mango chutney
2 sheets frozen puff pastry, thawed
1 egg white, lightly beaten

Combine the cream cheese, Cheddar cheese, green onions, curry powder and 1 1/2 tablespoons of the chutney in a bowl; mix well.

Roll 1 sheet of the pastry into a 12-inch square on a floured surface, trimming edges evenly. Cut into sixteen 3-inch squares.

Place 1 level teaspoon of the cheese filling in the center of each square. Top with 1/8 teaspoon of the remaining chutney.

Brush the pastry edges with egg white. Fold in half diagonally, forming a triangle. Press the edges with a fork to seal.

Arrange on a foil-lined baking sheet.

Repeat the process with the remaining pastry.

Bake at 400 degrees for 10 minutes.

Brush with the remaining 2 tablespoons chutney. Bake for 6 minutes longer.

These may be made ahead and stored, covered, in the refrigerator for 1 day or in the freezer for up to 1 month. Thaw before baking.

Duck Ravioli with Apple Cider Cream Sauce

yields 4 servings

For the filling

1 duck, split lengthwise
Salt and pepper to taste
2 large onions, chopped
10 cloves of garlic, chopped
1 cup butter

❧ Rinse the duck; season with salt and pepper.

❧ Sauté the onions and garlic in 1 tablespoon of the butter in a small skillet until tender.

❧ Place the duck, onions, garlic and remainder of the 1 cup butter in a roasting pan. Cover with foil.

❧ Bake at 250 degrees for 12 to 18 hours or until the meat falls off the bones. Remove the duck to a platter, reserving the pan drippings. Shred the meat finely, discarding the bones and skin.

For the ravioli

5 cups semolina flour
9 eggs
Salt to taste
1/4 cup water

❧ Combine the flour, eggs, salt and water in a large bowl.

❧ Knead until the dough is smooth and elastic.

❧ Let stand, covered, for 1 hour.

❧ Roll into thin sheets; cut into 2-inch circles. Cover and set aside.

Duck Ravioli with Apple Cider Cream Sauce
continued

For the sauce
4 cups apple cider
2 cups whipping cream
1 cup butter

❧ Strain the reserved pan drippings into a saucepan; set aside. Place the roasting pan on the burner. Add the apple cider.

❧ Cook until deglazed, stirring to scrape the bottom of the pan.

❧ Strain into the saucepan with the pan drippings. Cook until reduced to a syrupy consistency, stirring frequently.

❧ Add the whipping cream. Cook until reduced to the desired consistency, stirring frequently. Whip in the butter.

To assemble

❧ Brush the ravioli with water.

❧ Place 1 tablespoon of the duck filling on each circle; top with another circle, pressing the edge to seal.

❧ Cook in simmering water to cover in a large saucepan for 4 to 5 minutes; drain.

❧ Spoon into a serving bowl.

❧ Cover the ravioli with the cream sauce and serve immediately.

Marinated Meatballs

yields 24 meatballs

The meatballs are always a crowd pleaser. I'll never forget a wedding I catered. After the reception the bride's grandfather confessed to me that he had eaten thirty-two meatballs. Wow!

2 pounds lean ground beef
2 eggs, lightly beaten
2 medium onions, finely chopped
1 1/2 cups crushed cornflakes
1/2 cup water
1 teaspoon garlic powder
Salt and pepper to taste
1 (26-ounce) bottle catsup
1 1/4 cups water
1/4 cup Worcestershire sauce
1 1/2 cups packed brown sugar
2 bay leaves
1/2 cup golden raisins
1/2 teaspoon minced fresh rosemary

Combine the ground beef, eggs, onions, cornflakes, 1/2 cup water, garlic powder, salt and pepper in a medium bowl; mix well. Shape into 1-inch balls and set aside.

Mix the catsup, 1 1/4 cups water, Worcestershire sauce, brown sugar, bay leaves, raisins and rosemary in a large saucepan.

Cook over medium heat until the mixture begins to boil.

Add the meatballs to the sauce. Simmer over low heat for 1 hour, stirring occasionally. Discard the bay leaves.

Serve in a chafing dish to keep warm.

Purchased precooked meatballs may be substituted. Place in a baking pan and cover with the marinade sauce.

Bake at 350 degrees until hot and bubbly.

Pecan Cornmeal Breaded Oysters with Smoked Shallot Remoulade Sauce

yields 6 servings

For the sauce

3 shallots
2 cloves of garlic
1 red bell pepper
1 jalapeño
1 tablespoon vegetable oil
1 tablespoon cumin
1 tablespoon chili powder
1 bunch cilantro, chopped
Juice of 4 limes
2 gherkins, chopped
2 cups mayonnaise
Salt to taste

✺ Smoke the shallots, garlic, bell pepper and jalapeño. (See page 141 for instructions on Smoking.) Chop the vegetables finely.

✺ Place in a sauté pan with the oil, cumin and chili powder. Sauté over high heat for 20 seconds; remove from heat.

✺ Combine with the cilantro, lime juice, gherkins, mayonnaise and salt in a bowl; mix well.

✺ Chill, covered, for 3 hours.

For the oysters

20 oysters, shucked
2 cups flour
8 eggs, beaten
4 cups coarsely ground pecans
1 cup cornmeal
2 teaspoons salt
1/2 cup butter

✺ Dust the oysters with the flour. Dip in the eggs. Cover with a mixture of ground pecans, cornmeal and salt.

✺ Heat the butter in a sauté pan over high heat.

✺ Cook the oysters for 30 seconds on each side or until browned.

✺ Serve with the sauce.

Sausage and Sage Hand Pies

yields about 24 servings

*These miniature turnovers not only make a great hors d'oeuvre, but we often
make them larger and serve them as a daily special.*

1 small onion, finely chopped
2 pounds bulk sausage
3 tablespoons butter
2 medium potatoes, boiled, peeled, cubed
2 medium baking apples, peeled, chopped
3 tablespoons flour
1 tablespoon dark brown sugar
1/2 teaspoon salt
1 teaspoon freshly ground black pepper
1 tablespoon rubbed sage
Basic Pie Crust Dough, tripled (page 133)
2 egg yolks
2 tablespoons water

Sauté the onion and sausage in the butter in a skillet for 10 minutes or until browned.

Add the potatoes and apples. Sprinkle with the flour. Cook for 2 minutes longer.

Stir in the brown sugar, salt, pepper and sage; remove from heat.

Roll out the pastry 1/3 at a time to a 1/8-inch thickness. Cut into 2 1/2-inch circles.

Place a heaping teaspoon of the sausage mixture on one side of each circle. Moisten the edge with water; fold into a semicircle, pressing the edge to seal. Brush the surface with a mixture of the egg yolks and water. Place on ungreased baking sheets.

Bake at 350 degrees for 20 to 25 minutes or until golden brown. Serve warm.

Andrew's Eggnog

yields 10 to 12 cups

*Andrew makes this Christmas beverage every year and guests beg him for the recipe.
They can't believe it when he tells them the ingredients.*

1 half-gallon Blue Bell Homemade Vanilla Ice Cream (no substitutions, according to Andrew)
1 to 1½ cups bourbon, or to taste
Freshly ground nutmeg

Soften the ice cream in a large punch bowl.

Add the bourbon, stirring to blend.

Sprinkle with nutmeg. Serve well chilled.

Orange Spiced Iced Tea

yields 6 to 8 glasses

*We've served this as our house tea since the first day we opened. Our customers love its refreshing
flavor. We serve our glasses with a big slice of fresh orange.*

6 cups water
1 tea bag orange pekoe tea
2 tea bags Bigelow Constant Comment
Fresh orange slices

Bring 4 cups of the water to a boil in a saucepan.
Add the tea bags, steep for 5 to 10 minutes. Stir in the
remaining 2 cups water.

Serve over ice with fresh orange slices.

Strawberry Lemonade

yields 10 to 12 servings

*Texas summers can get really hot, and I love to make this refreshing
drink when the temperature starts to rise.*

1 cup fresh strawberries
1¹/₂ cups fresh lemon juice
1 cup maple syrup
7 to 8 cups water

Combine the strawberries, lemon juice and syrup in a blender container. Process until puréed.

Stir in the water. Serve over ice, garnished with fresh strawberries and fresh mint sprigs.

Soups

Soups

Chilled Avocado Soup, 39

Cantaloupe Soup, 40

Chilled Cucumber Soup, 41

Artichoke Cheddar Soup, 42

Black Bean Soup, 43

Chicken Tamale Soup, 44

The Dove's Nest White Chili, 45

Mexican Corn Soup with Grilled Shrimp and Cilantro Purée, 46

Roasted Eggplant Soup with Kalamata Olive Pesto, 48

Wild Mushroom and Smoked Gouda Soup, 50

Durham House Peanut Bisque, 51

Roasted Red Pepper Soup, 52

Fresh Squash and Cheese Soup, 53

Sweet Potato Soup with Caramelized Onions, 54

Texas Chowder, 55

Tomato Basil Soup, 56

Wild Rice Soup, 57

Creamy Zucchini Soup, 58

Chilled Avocado Soup

yields 10 to 12 servings

We serve a cup of this wonderful chilled soup with our Fresh Spinach Salad, found on page 74, and half of a sandwich to ladies' groups who book The Dove's Nest for luncheons in the spring and summer.

4 ripe avocados, peeled, seeded
1 clove of garlic, minced
4 green onions, chopped
5 tablespoons chopped fresh cilantro
1 to 2 tablespoons chopped jalapeños with juice
1/2 teaspoon Tabasco sauce
3 cups sour cream
1 cup buttermilk
8 cups chicken broth, chilled, fat removed
Salt and pepper to taste
Chopped green onions

Process the avocados, garlic, 4 green onions, cilantro, jalapeños and Tabasco sauce in a blender until smooth.

Add the sour cream. Process until blended.

Pour into a large bowl. Stir in the buttermilk and chicken broth. Season with salt and pepper.

Chill, covered, for several hours.

Ladle into soup bowls. Sprinkle with chopped green onions.

Cantaloupe Soup

yields 6 servings

This is simply wonderful. I serve it in beautiful, dainty teacups at ladies' luncheons and it makes a nice dessert soup served in half a cantaloupe.

2 medium ripe cantaloupes, cut into halves, seeded
$1/2$ cup sugar
$1/3$ cup fresh orange juice
1 tablespoon fresh lime juice
1 tablespoon fresh lemon juice
1 (8-ounce) can coconut milk
$1/4$ teaspoon vanilla extract
$1/8$ teaspoon ground ginger
$3/4$ cup half-and-half
Rum to taste

Scoop the pulp from the cantaloupes. Place in large bowl.

Add the sugar, orange juice, lime and lemon juices, coconut milk, vanilla, ginger, half-and-half and rum; mix well.

Pour half of the mixture into a blender container. Process for 2 to 3 minutes or until smooth. Repeat with the remaining mixture.

Pour into a large nonreactive bowl. Chill, covered, for several hours.

Ladle into teacups or soup bowls.

Chilled Cucumber Soup

yields 6 to 8 servings

3 unpeeled cucumbers
3 cups chicken stock
1½ cups sour cream
1¼ cups buttermilk
1½ tablespoons white wine vinegar
1 clove of garlic
½ cup chopped green onions
2 teaspoons salt
⅛ teaspoon freshly ground pepper
Toasted almond slivers

Place the cucumbers, chicken stock, sour cream, buttermilk, vinegar, garlic, green onions, salt and pepper in a blender container. Process until smooth.

Pour into a bowl. Cover the bowl and chill thoroughly.

Serve in soup bowls garnished with toasted almonds.

Artichoke Cheddar Soup

yields 12 servings

We have customers who will drop everything when they know I've made this for our
soup of the day. It has a wonderful velvety texture.

1 cup chopped onions
1 cup chopped carrots
1 cup chopped celery
$1/2$ cup butter
$1/2$ cup flour
2 tablespoons cornstarch
4 cups chicken broth
4 cups milk
2 cups shredded Cheddar cheese
1 teaspoon freshly ground pepper
2 (14-ounce) cans artichoke hearts, drained, cut into fourths
Salt to taste

Sauté the onions, carrots and celery in the butter in a stockpot until tender.

Stir in the flour and cornstarch. Add the chicken broth and milk.

Cook over medium heat until the mixture begins to boil and thicken, stirring frequently; reduce heat.

Add the cheese and pepper. Simmer until the cheese is melted, stirring frequently.

Stir in the artichoke hearts and salt.

Ladle the warm soup into soup bowls.

Black Bean Soup

yields 12 servings

A truly delicious soup with a Southwest flavor that has made this a very popular soup of the day.

4 cups dried black beans, sorted and rinsed
12 cups Basic Chicken Stock (page 136)
1 large onion, chopped
2 cloves of garlic, chopped
1 rib celery, chopped
1 (10-ounce) can tomatoes with green chiles
8 ounces ham hock or ham pieces
1 tablespoon cumin
3 tablespoons chopped cilantro
Juice of 1 lime
Salt and freshly ground pepper to taste
Shredded Monterey Jack cheese
Tortilla chips

Combine the beans, Basic Chicken Stock, onion, garlic, celery, tomatoes, ham, cumin and cilantro in a large stockpot.

Cook, covered, over low heat for 3 to 4 hours or until the beans are tender, stirring occasionally.

Pour into a food processor container in small batches. Process until puréed. Return to the stockpot.

Add the lime juice; season with salt and pepper. Cook just until heated through, stirring frequently. Add additional chicken stock if needed for desired consistency.

Ladle into soup bowls.

Serve garnished with shredded Monterey Jack cheese and tortilla chips.

Chicken Tamale Soup

yields 16 servings

The masa harina flour gives this soup a delicious tamale flavor. The soup is hearty enough to have as a meal, along with our Caesar Salad, found on page 69.

1/2 cup masa harina flour
1 1/2 cups water
12 cups chicken stock
3 cloves of garlic, minced
2 onions, chopped
2 tablespoons chili powder
1 tablespoon brown sugar
1 tablespoon dried oregano
2 tablespoons ground cumin
1 teaspoon freshly ground pepper
1 (8-ounce) can chopped green chiles
4 to 5 cups chopped cooked chicken
1 (15-ounce) can white hominy, drained
1 (15-ounce) can yellow hominy, drained
6 to 8 prepared tamales, cut into pieces
Salt to taste
Shredded Monterey Jack cheese

Mix the flour with the water in a large stockpot, stirring until smooth. Add the chicken stock.

Bring the mixture to a boil. Add the garlic, onions, chili powder, brown sugar, oregano, cumin, pepper and chiles.

Simmer, covered, for 15 minutes, stirring occasionally. Add the chicken and hominy.

Simmer for 20 minutes longer, stirring occasionally. Stir in the tamales and salt.

Ladle into soup bowls.

Serve garnished with shredded Monterey Jack cheese.

The Dove's Nest White Chili

yields 8 to 10 servings

This is without a doubt our number-one selling soup at the restaurant.
The Dallas Morning News even requested it for Dotty Griffith's food column.

2 tablespoons olive oil
1 medium onion, chopped
3 cloves of garlic, minced
2½ cups chopped fresh tomatoes, or 2 (10-ounce) cans tomatoes with green chiles, chopped
6 tomatillos, chopped
1 medium jalapeño, seeded, minced
2 cups chicken stock
1 (7-ounce) can chopped green chiles
2 cups chopped cooked chicken
½ teaspoon oregano
½ teaspoon cumin
¼ cup (heaping) chopped cilantro
2 (19-ounce) cans cannellini or Great Northern beans
1 tablespoon fresh lime juice
Salt and pepper to taste
Sour cream
Shredded Monterey Jack cheese
Fried tortilla strips

❦ Heat the olive oil in a large stockpot over medium-high heat. Add the onion. Sauté for 3 to 5 minutes or until softened. Add the garlic. Cook for 1 to 2 minutes longer; do not brown.

❦ Add the tomatoes, tomatillos and jalapeño. Cook until the tomatillos are tender, stirring occasionally.

❦ Add the chicken stock, green chiles, chicken, oregano, cumin, cilantro, beans and lime juice. Cook until heated through, stirring frequently. Season with salt and pepper.

❦ Ladle the chili into serving bowls.

❦ Serve garnished with a dollop of sour cream, shredded cheese and fried tortilla strips.

Mexican Corn Soup with
Grilled Shrimp and Cilantro Purée

yields 12 servings

One of the most requested soups on our dinner menu.

For the soup
1/2 cup butter
1 large onion, chopped
3 cloves of garlic, minced
1/2 gallon freshly cut corn
2 tablespoons brown sugar
2 tablespoons cumin
2 (4-ounce) cans green chiles
1 quart shrimp stock or bottled clam juice
1 yellow bell pepper, chopped
1/2 teaspoon pepper flakes
1 tablespoon oregano
1 cup whipping cream
1 (12-ounce) can beer (preferably imported), at room temperature
1 bunch fresh cilantro, chopped
Salt to taste

❧ Melt the butter in a large stockpot. Add the onion, garlic, corn, brown sugar and cumin.

❧ Sauté until the onion is translucent. Add the chiles, stock, bell pepper, pepper flakes and oregano. Bring to a boil.

❧ Cook for 10 minutes, stirring frequently; remove from heat.

❧ Purée the mixture in a blender; return to the stockpot.

❧ Stir in the cream, beer, cilantro and salt. Cover and keep warm.

Mexican Corn Soup with Grilled Shrimp and Cilantro Purée

continued

For the shrimp
Medium to large shrimp
Olive oil
Salt and pepper to taste

❧ Peel the shrimp to the last joint, leaving the last segment and tail intact; devein the shrimp.

❧ Brush the shrimp lightly with olive oil. Season with salt, pepper and/or any of your favorite herbs.

❧ Grill over hot coals until the shrimp turn pink, turning frequently.

For the cilantro purée
1 bunch cilantro
1 clove of garlic
1/4 cup vegetable oil
Juice of 1 lime
Salt to taste

❧ Combine the cilantro, garlic, oil, lime juice and salt in a blender container. Process the mixture until puréed.

To assemble

❧ Ladle the warm soup into soup bowls. Top with the shrimp.

❧ Pour the cilantro purée into a plastic squeeze bottle. Decorate each serving with a creative design.

Roasted Eggplant Soup with Kalamata Olive Pesto

yields 8 servings

I usually have to talk customers into trying this delicious soup, but they become instant fans after the first taste. Plus, it's very low in fat.

1 whole head of garlic, peeled
1 large onion, sliced into 1/2-inch rounds
4 red peppers, cut into halves and seeded
3 eggplants, cut into 1/2-inch rounds
1/2 cup olive oil
1 (8-ounce) can crushed tomatoes
4 cups strong chicken stock
1 teaspoon thyme
1 teaspoon oregano
2 tablespoons balsamic vinegar
Salt and pepper to taste
Kalamata Olive Pesto (page 49)

Arrange the garlic, onion, red peppers and eggplants on a large baking sheet. Brush with the olive oil. Roast at 400 degrees for 30 minutes.

Combine with the tomatoes, chicken stock, thyme, oregano and vinegar in a large stockpot. Bring to a boil. Cook for 10 minutes, stirring frequently.

Pour half the mixture into a blender container. Process until smooth. Repeat the process with the remaining mixture. Season with salt and pepper.

Ladle into soup bowls.

Serve garnished with a dollop of the olive pesto.

Kalamata Olive Pesto

yields 8 servings

1/2 cup kalamata olives, seeded
2 bunches fresh basil
1/4 cup feta or grated Parmesan cheese
1/4 cup pine nuts
1 cup olive oil
Salt and pepper to taste

Combine the olives, basil, cheese and pine nuts in a blender or food processor container.

Add the olive oil in a fine stream, processing constantly until of the desired consistency.

Season with salt and pepper. Pour into a covered container.

Store in the refrigerator.

Wild Mushroom and Smoked Gouda Soup

yields 12 servings

1/2 cup vegetable oil
2 cups chopped onions
6 cups sliced white mushrooms
6 cups sliced portobello or other wild mushrooms
12 roasted cloves of garlic
4 cups strong chicken stock
1 cup shredded smoked Gouda cheese or smoked Cheddar cheese
1 tablespoon sherry vinegar
1 cup whipping cream
1 teaspoon chopped thyme
1 teaspoon chopped basil
Salt and freshly ground pepper

Heat the oil in a medium stockpot. Sauté the onions, mushrooms and garlic in the oil for 10 minutes. Add the chicken stock.

Bring to a boil. Add the cheese, stirring until melted. Pour into a blender container.

Process until the mixture is puréed. Add the vinegar, cream, thyme, basil, salt and pepper. Process for 5 to 10 seconds to blend.

Ladle into soup bowls. Serve immediately.

Durham House Peanut Bisque

yields 8 to 10 servings

The Durham House was Waxahachie's finest restaurant for many years. A beautiful Victorian home a couple of blocks from the town square housed this institution, and back in the 1980s limousines would line up outside the house bringing hungry customers from miles around. The Durham House closed several years ago, but one of our dear friends and great customers, Mary Jo Blaine, gave me their famous recipe for Peanut Bisque. She said the owners gave it to her as a wedding gift when she and her husband held their rehearsal dinner there.

$1/2$ cup chopped celery
$1/2$ cup chopped onion
6 tablespoons unsalted butter
3 tablespoons flour
$41/2$ cups strong chicken stock
1 cup creamy peanut butter
$21/2$ cups half-and-half
$1/4$ teaspoon salt
$1/8$ teaspoon white pepper
1 teaspoon sweet paprika
3 drops of Tabasco sauce
Freshly chopped chives

Sauté the celery and onion in the butter in a skillet until tender. Transfer to a blender container. Process until smooth.

Pour the vegetable mixture into a large saucepan. Add the flour, stirring constantly with a wire whisk.

Cook over medium heat until blended, stirring constantly.

Whisk in the chicken stock gradually. Cook until the mixture begins to boil and thicken, whisking constantly.

Stir in the peanut butter, half-and-half, salt, pepper, paprika and Tabasco sauce.

Ladle into soup bowls. Garnish with chopped chives.

Roasted Red Pepper Soup

yields 10 to 12 servings

10 large red bell peppers
2 quarts strong chicken stock
1/4 cup sugar
2 cups whipping cream
Salt to taste

Arrange the red peppers on a baking sheet. Place on the top rack of the oven.

Broil until the skins become puffed and charred, turning as needed to blacken the entire surface. Place in a sealable plastic bag; seal tightly.

Let stand for several minutes to steam. Remove the red peppers from the bag and strip off the charred skin. Chop, discarding the stem and seeds.

Combine the red peppers and chicken stock in a large stockpot. Bring to a boil; remove from heat.

Process in a blender until the mixture is smooth. Return to the stockpot.

Add the sugar, cream and salt. Simmer gently until heated through, stirring frequently.

Ladle into soup bowls. Serve immediately.

Fresh Squash and Cheese Soup

yields 12 servings

4 cups thinly sliced zucchini
4 cups thinly sliced yellow squash
1 large onion, chopped
2 cloves of garlic, chopped
8 cups chicken stock
2 (10-ounce) cans cream of chicken soup
4 cups evaporated milk
4 cups shredded sharp Cheddar cheese
2 teaspoons dried oregano
2 tablespoons ground cumin
Salt and pepper to taste
Shredded Cheddar cheese
Bacon bits
Chopped green onions

Combine the zucchini, squash, onion, garlic and chicken stock in a large stockpot.

Cook over high heat until the mixture begins to boil, stirring occasionally.

Boil until the vegetables are tender; reduce heat.

Stir in the soup, evaporated milk, 4 cups cheese, oregano, cumin, salt and pepper. Simmer until the cheese is melted, stirring occasionally.

Ladle into soup bowls.

Garnish with additional shredded cheese, bacon bits and green onions.

Sweet Potato Soup with Caramelized Onions

yields 10 to 12 servings

1/2 cup butter
5 large yellow or white onions, thinly sliced
2 tablespoons brown sugar
4 sweet potatoes, cubed
2 quarts chicken stock
1/2 teaspoon allspice
1/2 teaspoon thyme
Salt and pepper to taste

Melt the butter in a large stockpot. Add the onions and brown sugar; mix well.

Cook over medium heat until the onions are browned and caramelized, stirring constantly.

Add the sweet potatoes, chicken stock, allspice, thyme, salt and pepper. Bring to a boil.

Cook for 20 to 30 minutes or until the sweet potatoes are tender.

Purée the mixture in a blender; return to the stockpot.

Ladle into soup bowls.

Texas Chowder

yields 10 to 12 servings

During the winter months, this is one of our most popular soups—a chowder hearty enough to be served as a one-course meal.

1 large onion, chopped
1 large red bell pepper, chopped
1 large green bell pepper, chopped
$^1/_2$ cup butter
1 (10-ounce) can cream of potato soup
$2^1/_2$ cups milk
1 tablespoon Worcestershire sauce
1 tablespoon chicken stock base
1 pound bulk sausage, browned
2 (17-ounce) cans cream-style corn
1 teaspoon crushed red pepper
2 cups shredded Cheddar cheese
$^1/_4$ cup chopped cilantro

Sauté the onion, red pepper and green pepper in the butter in a large stockpot until tender.

Add the potato soup, milk, Worcestershire sauce, chicken stock base, sausage, corn, red pepper, cheese and cilantro; mix well.

Simmer until the cheese is melted, stirring frequently.

Ladle into soup bowls.

Tomato Basil Soup

yields 12 servings

1 cup chopped onion
5 cloves of garlic, cut into halves
1/2 cup chopped bacon
1/4 cup olive oil
3 (28-ounce) cans whole tomatoes
2 cups chicken stock
2 teaspoons balsamic vinegar
1 cup whipping cream
1/2 cup chopped fresh basil
Salt and pepper to taste

❧ Sauté the onion, garlic and bacon in the olive oil in a large saucepan until the bacon is cooked through and the vegetables are tender.

❧ Add the tomatoes and chicken stock. Bring to a boil; remove from heat.

❧ Pour into a blender container. Process until the mixture is puréed.

❧ Stir in the vinegar, cream, basil, salt and pepper.

❧ Ladle into soup bowls. Serve immediately.

Wild Rice Soup

yields 12 servings

You may substitute three cans cream of potato soup for the potato-chicken stock purée.

2 large potatoes, peeled, cubed
3 cups chicken stock
9 slices bacon, cut into small pieces
1 medium onion, chopped
1½ cups wild rice, cooked
1 pint half-and-half
8 ounces Swiss cheese, shredded
Salt and freshly ground pepper to taste
Chopped green onions

Cook the potatoes in the chicken stock in a saucepan until the potatoes are tender. Pour into a food processor container. Process until puréed; set aside.

Sauté the bacon in a large saucepan. Add the onion and wild rice.

Cook until the onion is tender; reduce the heat.

Add the half-and-half, potato purée and cheese. Simmer over low heat until the cheese is melted, stirring constantly. Season with salt and pepper.

Ladle into soup bowls. Serve garnished with green onions

Creamy Zucchini Soup

yields 10 servings

2 medium onions, chopped
6 tablespoons butter
8 cups sliced zucchini
2 cups water or chicken broth
2 (10-ounce) cans cream of chicken soup
2 cups milk
2 cups half-and-half
2 tablespoons chopped fresh basil
Salt and pepper to taste

Sauté the onions in the butter in a large saucepan until tender. Add the zucchini and water.

Simmer for 30 minutes, stirring occasionally. Pour into a food processor container.

Process until smooth. Pour into the saucepan.

Stir in the chicken soup, milk, half-and-half, basil, salt and pepper.

Cook over very low heat until heated through, stirring constantly.

Ladle into soup bowls.

SALADS & DRESSINGS

Salads and Dressings

Curried Chicken and Wild Rice Salad, 61

Grilled Chicken and Black Bean Salad, 62

Hot Chicken Salad in Puff Pastry, 63

Southwestern Pasta Salad with Smoked Chicken and
Oven-Dried Cherry Tomatoes, 64

The Dove's Nest Chicken Apricot Salad, 65

Vietnamese Chicken Salad, 66

Turkey, Red Grape and Bleu Cheese Salad with
Honey Tabasco Dressing, 67

Smoked Turkey and Artichoke Salad with
Green Peppercorn and Tarragon Mayonnaise, 68

The Dove's Nest Caesar Salad, 69

Baby Field Greens with Candied Walnuts, Bacon and Goat Cheese
in a Balsamic Maple Vinaigrette, 70

Wild Mushroom and Boursin Salad, 71

Grilled New Potato Salad with Warm Bacon, Balsamic and
Roasted Shallot Vinaigrette, 72

Hill Country Potato Salad, 73

Fresh Spinach Salad with Orange Curry Dressing, 74

The Dove's Nest Tortellini Salad, 75

Tortilla and Jicama Slaw with Cilantro Lime and
Cotija Cheese Vinaigrette, 76

Curried Chicken and Wild Rice Salad

yields 12 servings

*I've served this salad many times for ladies' luncheons—it's always a winner.
Smoked turkey may be substituted for the chicken.*

For the dressing

2 cloves of garlic
3 tablespoons white wine vinegar
1/4 cup fresh lemon juice
3 tablespoons mango chutney
1 1/2 tablespoons curry powder
2/3 cup olive oil
3/4 cup sour cream
3 tablespoons water

Process the garlic, vinegar, lemon juice, chutney and curry powder in a blender. Add the olive oil in a slow stream, processing constantly until thickened.

Add the sour cream and water. Process until blended.

For the salad

3 cups wild rice blend, cooked
4 pounds chopped cooked chicken
1 cup sliced almonds, toasted
1 cup golden raisins
1 bunch green onions, chopped

Combine the wild rice, chicken, almonds, raisins and green onions in a large salad bowl; mix well.

Pour the dressing over the salad. Toss gently to coat.

Grilled Chicken and Black Bean Salad

yields 4 to 6 servings

A great Southwest salad and very colorful.

2 (8-ounce) grilled chicken breasts, thinly sliced
1 (16-ounce) can black beans, drained
1 small red onion, chopped
1 red bell pepper, chopped
2 tomatoes, peeled, seeded, chopped
1/4 cup chopped cilantro
1/3 cup olive oil
1/4 cup red wine vinegar
3 cloves of garlic, chopped
6 corn tortillas, torn into thin strips
Corn oil for frying

Combine the chicken, beans, onion, red pepper, tomatoes and cilantro in a large bowl; mix well.

Mix the olive oil, vinegar and garlic in a 2-cup measure. Pour over the salad, tossing to coat.

Marinate in the refrigerator for 2 hours.

Fry the tortilla strips in corn oil in a skillet until crispy; drain. Toss with the salad just before serving.

Hot Chicken Salad in Puff Pastry

yields 8 servings

We have served this for years as a bridal brunch entrée with our Fresh Spinach Salad, found on page 74. It's fun to cut the puff pastry top out with a heart-shape cookie cutter.

8 ounces chopped cooked chicken breasts
2 ribs celery, chopped
1 onion, chopped
1/2 cup sliced mushrooms
3 tablespoons chopped pimentos
1/4 cup sliced almonds, toasted
3 hard-cooked eggs, chopped
1 cup mayonnaise
2 cups cream of chicken soup
1/2 cup shredded Cheddar cheese
1/2 teaspoon chicken soup base
2 tablespoons curry powder
1 1/2 teaspoons Cavender's Greek Seasoning
Freshly ground pepper to taste
8 puff pastry shells

❧ Combine the chicken, celery, onion, mushrooms, pimentos, almonds, eggs, mayonnaise, soup, cheese, soup base, curry powder, Greek seasoning and pepper in a bowl; mix well.

❧ Spoon into an ungreased 9x13-inch baking pan.

❧ Bake at 350 degrees for 30 minutes or until hot and bubbly.

❧ Bake the puff pastry shells using package directions.

❧ Fill the shells with the hot chicken mixture.

❧ Serve immediately.

Southwestern Pasta Salad with Smoked Chicken and Oven-Dried Cherry Tomatoes

yields 6 to 8 servings

For the dressing

2 tablespoons chopped fresh cilantro
1 tablespoon chopped fresh thyme
1 tablespoon chopped fresh basil
1 clove of garlic, minced
2 shallots, minced
1 tablespoon dry white wine
2 tablespoons white wine vinegar
1 tablespoon balsamic vinegar
1/2 cup olive oil
1/4 cup corn oil
Salt and freshly ground pepper

For the salad

9 ounces fusilli or penne
Salt to taste
3 tablespoons olive oil
1/2 cup canned black beans, drained
1/2 medium red bell pepper, cut into 1/4-inch strips
1/2 medium yellow bell pepper, cut into 1/4-inch strips
1 small carrot, coarsely chopped
5 tomatillos, cored and cut into 1/4-inch cubes
4 ounces mozzarella cheese, cut into 1/3-inch cubes
1 (8-ounce) boneless smoked chicken breast,
cut into 1/3-inch cubes (page 141)
1 cup oven-dried cherry tomatoes (page 139)
1 tablespoon chopped fresh basil
1 clove of garlic, minced

Combine the cilantro, thyme, basil, garlic and shallots in a small bowl. Whisk in the wine and the vinegars.

Add the olive oil and corn oil in a fine stream, whisking constantly.

Season to taste with salt and pepper; set aside.

Cook the pasta in boiling salted water until al dente; drain. Place in a large serving bowl. Toss with the olive oil. Set aside until cool.

Stir in the black beans, red and yellow peppers, carrot, tomatillos, cheese, chicken, tomatoes, basil and garlic. Toss with the dressing. Adjust the seasonings.

Chill, covered, for 20 minutes. The salad may be made up to 3 hours before serving time.

The Dove's Nest Chicken Apricot Salad
yields 12 servings

I've been making this salad since the first day we opened. It immediately became a hit.
We have some customers who have never tried anything else on the menu because they love it so much.

For the dressing
2 large egg yolks
2 tablespoons fresh lemon juice
2 tablespoons grainy Dijon mustard
3 tablespoons chopped fresh rosemary
3/4 cup vegetable oil
2/3 cup olive oil
1/4 cup honey mustard
Salt and freshly ground pepper to taste

❧ Process the egg yolks, lemon juice, mustard and rosemary in a food processor fitted with a steel blade for 10 minutes.

❧ Add the vegetable and olive oils in a fine stream, processing constantly until thickened.

❧ Add the honey mustard, salt and pepper. Process until smooth; set aside.

For the salad
3 pounds cooked boneless skinless chicken breasts
1 cup dried apricots, cut into 1/4-inch strips
1/3 cup sherry
3 ribs celery, chopped
Green tops from 4 scallions, chopped
1/2 cup sliced almonds, toasted

❧ Shred the chicken into a large bowl.

❧ Combine the apricots and sherry in a small saucepan. Simmer for 3 minutes to plump the apricots. Add to the chicken.

❧ Add the celery, scallions and almonds to the chicken mixture, stirring gently.

❧ Add the salad dressing, tossing to coat.

Vietnamese Chicken Salad

yields 8 to 10 servings

This is one of my favorite salads. It's so fresh and the marinated grilled chicken is nothing short of addictive. Marinated grilled pork tenderloin may be substituted for chicken.

For the marinade
1/2 cup soy sauce
2 cloves of garlic, minced
8 teaspoons sugar
2 tablespoons sherry
4 teaspoons hoisin sauce

Mix 1/2 cup soy sauce, 2 cloves of garlic, 8 teaspoons sugar, sherry and hoisin sauce in a small bowl.

For the salad
6 boneless chicken breasts
2 heads iceberg lettuce, shredded
2 bunches each green onions and fresh cilantro, chopped
1/2 cup toasted peanuts or cashews
1/4 cup toasted sesame seeds

Rinse the chicken and pat dry. Place in a shallow dish. Add the soy sauce mixture, turning to coat.

Marinate, covered, in the refrigerator for 24 hours, turning occasionally. Drain, discarding the marinade.

Grill the chicken over hot coals until cooked through. Let stand until cool. Cut into strips.

Toss with the lettuce, 2 bunches green onions, cilantro, peanuts and sesame seeds in a large bowl.

For the dressing
1/2 cup sesame oil
1/2 white wine vinegar
1/4 cup soy sauce
5 tablespoons sugar
2 teaspoons crushed red pepper
6 cloves of garlic, minced
2 green onions, chopped

Whisk the sesame oil and vinegar in a small bowl until combined. Add 1/4 cup soy sauce, 5 tablespoons sugar, red pepper, 6 cloves of garlic and 2 green onions; mix well.

Pour over the salad, tossing to coat.

Turkey, Red Grape and
Honey Taba...

yields 4

This salad will keep in the refrigerator for several days.

For the dressing
1/2 cup vegetable oil
1/2 cup chopped onion
1/4 cup white wine vinegar
1/4 cup honey
2 teaspoons Tabasco sauce
Salt and pepper to taste

Combine the oil, onion, wine vinegar, honey and Tabasco sauce in a blender container.

Process until smooth.

Season with salt and pepper.

For the salad
8 ounces smoked turkey, cubed
2/3 cup crumbled bleu cheese
2/3 cup coarsely chopped pecans, toasted
1 cup red seedless grapes

Combine the turkey, bleu cheese, pecans and grapes in a salad bowl and mix gently.

Add the dressing, tossing to coat.

Smoked Turkey and Artichoke Salad with Green Peppercorn and Tarragon Mayonnaise
yields 10 servings

For the mayonnaise
2 large egg yolks
1 large egg
1/2 tablespoon Dijon mustard
1/2 tablespoon green peppercorns
packed in brine, drained
2 1/2 tablespoons chopped fresh tarragon
3 tablespoons fresh lemon juice
1 1/4 cups olive oil
1 1/2 cups vegetable oil
Salt to taste

✺ Process the egg yolks, egg, mustard, peppercorns, tarragon and lemon juice in a blender until smooth.

✺ Add the oils in a fine stream, processing constantly until the mayonnaise is of the desired consistency. Season with salt.

For the salad
3 pounds smoked turkey, cubed
1 large red onion, chopped
2 (16-ounce) cans artichoke hearts, drained
4 ribs celery, chopped
Freshly ground pepper

✺ Combine the turkey, onion, artichokes and celery in a medium bowl; mix well. Season with pepper.

✺ Add the prepared mayonnaise. Toss gently to coat.

✺ Spoon into a salad bowl.

The Dove's Nest Caesar Salad

yields 12 servings

For the dressing

4 cloves of garlic
6 anchovy fillets
2 teaspoons Worcestershire sauce
4 egg yolks
2 tablespoons Dijon mustard
2/3 cup red wine vinegar
2²/3 cups olive oil

❧ Combine the garlic, anchovies, Worcestershire sauce, egg yolks, Dijon mustard and vinegar in a blender container.

❧ Process until smooth.

❧ Add the olive oil in a fine stream, processing constantly until thickened.

For the salad

1 loaf French or sourdough bread, cut into small cubes
1/4 cup melted butter
1/4 cup olive oil
3 heads Romaine lettuce, torn into bite-size pieces
1 cup freshly grated Parmesan cheese
Freshly ground pepper to taste

❧ Spread the bread cubes on a baking sheet. Drizzle a mixture of the melted butter and olive oil evenly over the bread.

❧ Bake at 375 degrees for 15 to 20 minutes or until browned and crisp; cool. Reserve 2 to 3 cups of the croutons for the salad; store the remaining croutons in a sealed container.

❧ Combine the lettuce, cheese, pepper and the reserved croutons in a salad bowl. Add the dressing, tossing to coat.

Baby Field Greens with Candied Walnuts, Bacon and Goat Cheese in a Balsamic Maple Vinaigrette

yields 8 servings

This is our house dressing that is delicious with any mixed greens, but this combination is especially good.

For the candied walnuts

1/4 cup packed brown sugar
1 cup walnut halves
2 tablespoons water

❧ Cook the brown sugar in a large heavy skillet over medium-high heat until melted.

❧ Add the walnuts and water. Cook for 10 minutes or until the water evaporates, stirring constantly.

❧ Spread the walnuts on a sheet pan and let stand to dry.

❧ Store in an airtight container.

For the vinaigrette

1 cup balsamic vinegar
1/2 cup pure maple syrup
1/4 cup minced shallots
3 cups olive oil
2 teaspoons salt
1 teaspoon pepper

❧ Combine the vinegar, syrup, shallots, olive oil, salt and pepper in a jar with a tightfitting lid.

❧ Shake vigorously to mix; chill.

For the salad APPLES?

8 cups assorted baby field greens, such as endive, radicchio, frisée, red oak leaf or spinach
12 slices bacon, crisp-fried, crumbled
1/2 cup crumbled goat cheese

❧ Mix the greens, bacon, cheese and walnuts in a large salad bowl.

❧ Drizzle 1/2 cup of the vinaigrette over the salad, tossing gently to coat.

Wild Mushroo...

yi...

2 pounds wild mushroom...
2 ta...
Salt and pepper to taste
8 cups mixed field greens, such as endive, radicchio, frisée, red oak leaf or spinach
6 ounces boursin cheese, crumbled
2 roasted red bell peppers, cut into julienne strips (page 140)
1 cup Balsamic Maple Vinaigrette (page 70)

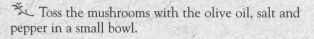

Toss the mushrooms with the olive oil, salt and pepper in a small bowl.

Grill over medium-hot coals until brown or done to taste. Place in a bowl.

Chill, covered, in the refrigerator.

Combine the mixed greens, cheese and red peppers in a salad bowl and mix gently.

Drizzle with the Balsamic Maple Vinaigrette, tossing to coat.

Grilled New Potato Salad with
Warm Bacon, Balsamic and Roasted Shallot Vinaigrette

yields 8 servings

For the vinaigrette

10 shallots
2 tablespoons olive oil
1 pound bacon, chopped
2 cups balsamic vinegar
1 tablespoon freshly ground pepper
Salt to taste

❧ Arrange the shallots on a baking sheet. Drizzle with the olive oil. Roast at 350 degrees for 30 minutes; set aside.

❧ Fry the bacon in a large skillet until crispy. Drain, reserving the pan drippings.

❧ Process the shallots, bacon, vinegar and pepper in a blender. Add the reserved pan drippings gradually, processing until smooth. Season with salt.

For the salad

8 cups new potatoes, cut into quarters
1 to 2 tablespoons vegetable oil
8 cups mixed greens, such as spinach, turnip greens, mustard greens, endive or radicchio

❧ Boil the potatoes in a saucepan with water to cover for 10 minutes. Drain and cool.

❧ Brush the potatoes with the oil. Grill over medium-hot coals for 10 minutes or until tender.

❧ Pour the prepared vinaigrette into a saucepan. Heat over low heat until warmed through. Add the potatoes and remove from heat.

❧ Toss the potatoes and dressing with the mixed greens in a large salad bowl. Serve immediately.

Hill Country Potato Salad

yields 12 servings

A great alternative to the old traditional potato salad, and much lower in fat!

For the dressing

²/₃ cup vegetable oil
¹/₃ cup cider vinegar
¹/₄ cup fresh lemon juice
4 pickled jalapeños
4 cloves of garlic
1 teaspoon ground cumin
1 teaspoon dried oregano
1 teaspoon freshly ground pepper
1 teaspoon salt
¹/₄ cup chopped fresh cilantro

Combine the oil, vinegar, lemon juice, jalapeños, garlic, cumin, oregano, pepper, salt and cilantro in a blender container.

Process at high speed until smooth.

For the salad

6 red potatoes, unpeeled, cut into quarters
1 red onion, sliced
1 cup whole kernel corn, canned or frozen
2 red bell peppers, cut into julienne strips
6 green onions, chopped

Cook the potatoes in boiling water in a saucepan until tender; drain.

Toss with the dressing in a large bowl.

Add the onion, corn, red peppers and green onions, tossing to coat.

Serve chilled or at room temperature.

Fresh Spinach Salad with Orange Curry Dressing

yields 12 servings

A very colorful salad and one of our most popular. Hardly a day goes by that a customer doesn't request the recipe for our Orange Curry Dressing.

For the dressing

1 cup cider vinegar
2 tablespoons (heaping) orange marmalade
2 teaspoons curry powder
1/2 cup sugar
2 teaspoons dry mustard
2 teaspoons salt
1 teaspoon freshly ground pepper
1/2 teaspoon Tabasco sauce
1 3/4 cups vegetable oil

Combine the vinegar, marmalade, curry powder, sugar, mustard, salt, pepper and Tabasco sauce in a blender container.

Add the oil in a fine stream, processing constantly at high speed until thickened.

Let stand at room temperature for 2 hours. Chill, covered, in the refrigerator until serving time.

For the salad

4 bunches fresh spinach, trimmed
6 Red Delicious apples, chopped
2 cups golden raisins
1 3/4 cups walnut halves
6 green onions, chopped
1/4 cup sesame seeds, toasted
1 pound bacon, chopped, crisp-fried, crumbled

Arrange equal amounts of the spinach on 12 salad plates. Drizzle with the dressing.

Sprinkle each serving with the apples, raisins, walnuts, green onions, sesame seeds and bacon bits.

Serve immediately.

The Dove's Nest Tortellini Salad

yields 10 servings

*A very colorful and fresh-tasting salad. Makes a nice presentation to serve
for company or to take on a summer gathering.*

For the dressing

1 egg yolk
2 tablespoons fresh lemon juice
1 tablespoon Dijon mustard
1 tablespoon balsamic vinegar
1 cup vegetable oil
1/2 cup olive oil
1 teaspoon dried thyme
Zest of 1 orange
Salt and freshly ground pepper to taste

Process the egg yolk in a food processor for 5
seconds. Add the lemon juice, mustard and vinegar.

Add the oils in a fine stream, processing constantly
until thickened. Add the thyme, orange zest, salt and
pepper. Process until smooth.

For the salad

2 pounds tri-color tortellini, cooked,
drained, cooled
1 head broccoli, cut into florets, blanched
1 pound carrots, sliced diagonally, blanched
3 leeks, white part only, sliced
1 red bell pepper, cut into julienne strips
1 yellow bell pepper, cut into julienne strips
1/2 cup fresh chopped basil

Combine the tortellini, broccoli, carrots, leeks, bell
peppers and basil in a large salad bowl. Pour the dressing
over the vegetables. Toss gently to coat.

The salad may be served immediately, but the
flavor is enhanced if prepared 24 hours before serving.

Tortilla and Jicama Slaw with Cilantro Lime and Cotija Cheese Vinaigrette

yields 8 servings

This crunchy, fresh slaw is a wonderful alternative to the traditional slaw. We serve it on our dinner menu with fried oysters. I like to make it as an accompanied salad when we have our annual crawfish boil.

For the vinaigrette

1 clove of garlic
1 shallot
Juice of 10 fresh limes
1 bunch cilantro
1/2 cup shredded cotija cheese or crumbled feta cheese
Salt to taste
3/4 cup vegetable or canola oil

Combine the garlic, shallot, lime juice, cilantro, cheese and salt in a blender container.

Add the oil in a fine stream, processing constantly at high speed until thickened.

For the slaw

3 cups tortillas, cut into thin strips
Corn oil for frying
1 medium jicama, peeled, cut into thin strips
1/2 cup shredded green cabbage
1/2 cup shredded red cabbage
1/2 cup grated carrot
1 red bell pepper, cut into julienne strips
1 yellow bell pepper, cut into julienne strips

Deep-fry the tortilla strips in oil until browned and crispy. Drain on paper towels and set aside.

Combine the jicama, cabbage, carrot and bell peppers in a large salad bowl.

Add the prepared vinaigrette, tossing to coat. May prepare up to 1 hour ahead, adding the tortilla strips just before serving.

The jicama is peeled by slicing off the top and bottom with a sharp knife, then peeling by hand.

Entrées and Side Dishes

Grilled Lamb Chops with Mole Rojo Sauce and Goat Cheese Whipped Potatoes, 79

Pork Tenderloin with Bleu Cheese Bacon Whipped Potatoes and
Dried Cherry Port Demi-Glace Sauce, 80

The Dove's Nest Flowerpot Chicken Pie, 82

Herb-Crusted Chicken with Mustard Butter, 83

Pecan-Smoked Chicken Breast with Jalapeño Monterey Jack Cheese Spoon Bread,
Peach and Strawberry Tequila Salsa and Balsamic Lime Reduction, 84

Risotto with Smoked Chicken, Oven-Dried Tomatoes, Brie,
Asparagus Tips and Pine Nuts, 86

The Dove's Nest Chicken Soufflé, 87

Chicken Zucchini Quiche, 88

Southwest Quiche, 89   Southwest Strata, 90

Southwestern Crab Meat Soufflé, 91

Grilled Mahimahi with Red Onion Couscous and Chunky
Papaya-Avocado-Citrus Vinaigrette, 92

Smoked Salmon and Goat Cheese Quiche, 93

Salmon with Chipotle Sesame Vinaigrette and Fried Basmati Rice with Shellfish, 94

Pecan-Crusted Rainbow Trout, Scalloped Sweet Potatoes and
Smoked Tangerine Butter Sauce, 96

Sourdough-Breaded Rainbow Trout with Buttermilk and
Chive Whipped Potatoes and Smoked Crawfish Sauce, 98

Seared Ahi Tuna with Thai Salad and Fried Rice Noodles, 100

Buttermilk, Wild Rice and Pecan Pancakes, 101

Wild Mushroom and Three-Cheese Lasagna, 102

Portobello Mushrooms, Scallops and Goat Cheese Manicotti with Red Pepper Coulis, 104

Onion Tart, 105

Nutted Wild Rice, 106

Southwestern Squash Casserole, 107

Vegetable Casserole with Goat Cheese and Herbs, 108

Grilled Lamb Chops with Mole Rojo Sauce and Goat Cheese Whipped Potatoes

yields 4 servings

For the sauce

1 recipe Veal Demi-Glace (page 137)
1 cup prepared mole sauce

Prepare a veal demi-glace, substituting lamb bones for veal bones. Mix 1 cup of the demi-glace with 1 cup of prepared mole sauce.

For the lamb chops

3 racks of lamb, French-cut
Cavander's Greek seasoning to taste

Slice the lamb between the bones. Wrap the ends of the bones with foil. Sprinkle with the seasoning.

Grill over medium-hot coals for 3 to 4 minutes per side.

For the potatoes

3 potatoes, peeled, cubed
2 to 3 tablespoons butter
1/4 cup whipping cream
1/2 cup crumbled goat cheese
Salt and freshly ground pepper to taste

Boil the potatoes in water to cover in a saucepan until tender. Drain well.

Beat the potatos in a mixer bowl until fluffy. Add the butter, cream, cheese, salt and pepper, beating until smooth.

To assemble

Spoon a mound of the potatoes in the center of each of 4 serving plates. Arrange 6 lamb chops in a circle around the potatoes with the bones pointing up. Drizzle the sauce around the edge of the plates.

Pork Tenderloin with
Bleu Cheese Bacon Whipped Potatoes and
Dried Cherry Port Demi-Glace Sauce

yields 12 servings

For the sauce

1/4 cup dried cherries
1/4 cup port
1 cup Veal Demi-Glace (page 137)
Salt and pepper to taste

❧ Combine the cherries, wine, demi-glace, salt and pepper in a small saucepan.

❧ Simmer over low heat until heated through, stirring frequently.

For the tenderloin

6 (1 1/2- to 1 3/4-pound) pork tenderloins
Salt and pepper to taste

❧ Season the tenderloins with salt and pepper.

❧ Grill over medium-low coals until cooked through, turning occasionally.

❧ Slice each tenderloin into 10 medallions.

Pork Tenderloin with
Bleu Cheese Bacon Whipped Potatoes and
Dried Cherry Port Demi~Glace Sauce
continued

For the potatoes

5 potatoes, peeled, cubed
1/4 cup butter
1/2 cup whipping cream
1 cup crumbled bleu cheese
10 slices bacon, crisp-fried, crumbled
Salt and pepper to taste.

❧ Cook the potatoes in water in a saucepan until tender; drain.

❧ Beat with an electric mixer until fluffy. Add the butter, cream, cheese, bacon, salt and pepper, beating until well mixed.

To assemble

❧ Spoon a mound of potatoes in the center of each of 12 serving plates.

❧ Fan the pork medallions around the potatoes. Spoon the sauce over the pork.

The Dove's Nest Flowerpot Chicken Pie

yields 12 servings

Thursdays at The Dove's Nest means Potpie Day, and our customers start calling early in the morning to reserve one in case we run out before they get seated. Most tell us that it's the best chicken potpie they have ever tasted.

1 whole chicken
4 cups water or chicken stock
1 each bay leaf and clove of garlic
3 cups thinly sliced carrots
2 cups cubed peeled potatoes
1 cup finely chopped onion
1/2 cup sherry
1 tablespoon finely chopped fresh basil
1 cup sliced mushrooms
2 cups green peas
1/2 cup each butter and flour
2 cups whipping cream
Salt and freshly ground pepper to taste
3 recipes Basic Pie Crust Dough (page 133)
3 egg yolks, beaten

Rinse the chicken. Boil the chicken in water with the bay leaf and garlic in a large stockpot until cooked through. Remove the chicken from the stockpot, reserving the stock. Let the chicken cool and then debone. Add the carrots, potatoes, onion and sherry to the reserved stock. Cook over medium-high heat until the vegetables are tender. Add the basil, mushrooms and peas. Cook for 5 minutes longer. Discard the bay leaf.

Melt the butter in a medium saucepan. Stir in the flour gradually. Pour in the cream gradually, stirring until mixed. Simmer until thickened, stirring constantly.

Add the cream mixture and chicken to the vegetables and broth, stirring well. Simmer until mixture thickens. Season with salt and pepper. Roll out the pie pastry to a 1/8-inch thickness. Cut into 12 six-inch circles. Fill 12 flowerpots or large ramekins with the chicken mixture. Top with a pastry circle. Brush the tops with the beaten egg yolks.

Bake at 350 degrees for 30 minutes or until browned and bubbly.

Herb-Crusted Chicken with Mustard Butter

yields 4 servings

The mustard butter may be made up to two weeks in advance and kept chilled.

For the mustard butter
1/2 cup unsalted butter, softened
2 tablespoons minced shallot
1/2 teaspoon white pepper
3/4 teaspoon coarse salt
1 1/2 tablespoons chopped fresh thyme
2 tablespoons coarse-grained mustard
2 tablespoons Dijon mustard

Combine the butter, shallot, pepper, salt, thyme and mustards in a bowl. Beat until light and fluffy.

Shape the butter into a 7-inch log on waxed paper. Wrap in the waxed paper. Chill until firm.

For the chicken
4 (8-ounce) boneless chicken breasts
1 teaspoon crumbled dried sage
1 teaspoon crumbled dried oregano
1 teaspoon ground ginger
1 teaspoon crumbled dried rosemary
1 teaspoon crumbled dried marjoram
1 teaspoon crumbled dried thyme
1 teaspoon celery seeds
1 teaspoon white pepper
2 teaspoons coarse salt
2 tablespoons butter

Rinse the chicken and pat dry. Combine the sage, oregano, ginger, rosemary, marjoram, thyme, celery seeds, pepper and salt in a shallow bowl. Coat the chicken in the herb mixture.

Sauté the chicken in butter in a large skillet for 5 minutes on each side or until cooked through.

Arrange the chicken on serving plates. Serve with a slice of mustard butter on top.

Pecan-Smoked Chicken Breast with Jalapeño Monterey Jack Cheese Spoon Bread, Peach and Strawberry Tequila Salsa and Balsamic Lime Reduction

yields 6 servings

For the chicken

6 (8-ounce) chicken breasts
3/4 cup vegetable oil
6 tablespoons chopped garlic
1 tablespoon salt

Rinse the chicken and pat dry. Combine the vegetable oil, garlic and salt in a shallow bowl; mix well. Add the chicken. Marinate, covered, in the refrigerator overnight.

Cold smoke the chicken. (See page 141 for instructions on Smoking.)

Grill the chicken over medium-hot coals until cooked through, turning occasionally.

For the salsa

6 peaches, chopped
1 pint strawberries, chopped
1/2 cup chopped red onion
1 tablespoon minced jalapeño
1 tablespoon dark chili powder
1 bunch cilantro, chopped
1 tablespoon tequila
Juice of 4 limes
Juice of 4 oranges

Mix the peaches, strawberries, red onion, jalapeño, chili powder, cilantro, tequila, lime juice and orange juice in a medium bowl.

Chill, covered, in the refrigerator.

Pecan-Smoked Chicken Breast with Jalapeño Monterey Jack Cheese Spoon Bread, Peach and Strawberry Tequila Salsa and Balsamic Lime Reduction

continued

For the balsamic lime reduction

2 cups balsamic vinegar
Juice of 2 limes

❧ Simmer the vinegar in a nonreactive saucepan until reduced by two-thirds. Remove from heat.

❧ Stir in the lime juice. Let stand until cool. Pour into a squeeze bottle.

For the spoon bread

5 cloves of garlic, minced
1 cup chopped onion
2 1/4 cups milk
2 1/4 cups chicken stock
1 1/2 cups cornmeal
5 cups shredded jalapeño Monterey Jack cheese
1 (8-ounce) can green chiles, drained
1/2 cup maple syrup
Salt to taste
6 egg yolks, beaten
6 egg whites

❧ Combine the garlic, onion, milk and chicken stock in a medium saucepan. Bring to a boil. Stir in the cornmeal.

❧ Cook over medium heat for 15 to 20 minutes or until thickened, stirring frequently. Remove from heat. Add the cheese, chiles, syrup, salt and egg yolks, mixing well.

❧ Beat the egg whites in a mixer bowl until stiff peaks form. Fold into the batter. Pour into a 9x12-inch greased baking pan.

❧ Bake at 350 degrees for 1 hour and 20 minutes.

To assemble

❧ Place a chicken breast and a serving of spoon bread on each individual serving plate. Spoon the salsa on top of the chicken.

❧ Garnish by squeezing designs of balsamic lime reduction over the entire plate.

Risotto with Smoked Chicken, Oven-Dried Tomatoes, Brie, Asparagus Tips and Pine Nuts

yields 4 servings

2 cups Basic Chicken Stock (page 136)
4 cups water
2 teaspoons olive oil
2 cups arborio rice
1/2 cup dry white wine
4 smoked chicken breasts, sliced (page 141)
1 cup Oven-Dried Tomatoes (page 139)
1/4 cup pine nuts, toasted
1 cup cubed Brie cheese
1 bunch fresh asparagus, tips only, blanched
1/4 cup chopped fresh basil
Salt and freshly ground pepper to taste

Combine the chicken stock and water in a large saucepan. Bring to a boil over high heat; reduce heat. Simmer gently to keep warm.

Heat the olive oil in a nonreactive medium saucepan. Add the rice. Cook over medium heat for 1 minute, stirring until the rice is coated.

Stir in the white wine. Cook until absorbed.

Add the warmed chicken broth mixture 1 cup at a time, being sure that all liquid is absorbed before adding more.

Cook over medium heat for 18 minutes or until rice is tender but firm, stirring constantly.

Add the chicken, tomatoes, pine nuts, Brie cheese, asparagus tips, basil, salt and pepper; mix well. Serve immediately.

The Dove's Nest Chicken Soufflé

yields 12 servings

*This is a recipe I began preparing when I first started making lunch in the back of my mom's gift shop.
It makes a nice luncheon entrée served with our Fresh Spinach Salad, found on page 74.*

16 slices white bread, crusts trimmed
2½ pounds chicken breasts, cooked, cut into small pieces
8 ounces sliced black olives
5 hard-cooked eggs, chopped
8 ounces mushrooms, sliced
2 green onions, chopped
1½ cups mayonnaise
1 tablespoon curry powder
½ tablespoon garlic powder
Salt and freshly ground pepper to taste
2 (10-ounce) cans cream of chicken soup
2 cups sour cream

Line a 9x13-inch glass baking dish with half the bread.

Mix the chicken, olives, eggs, mushrooms, green onions, mayonnaise, curry powder, garlic powder, salt and pepper in a bowl. Spoon evenly over the bread; top with the remaining bread.

Combine the soup and sour cream in a small bowl; mix well. Spread over the bread layer. Chill, covered, overnight.

Bake at 350 degrees for 1 hour. Let stand for 10 to 15 minutes. Cut into squares to serve.

Chicken Zucchini Quiche

yields 8 servings

The addition of cream cheese makes this quiche wonderfully rich and creamy in texture.

1/2 recipe Basic Pie Crust Dough (page 133)
3 medium zucchini, grated
1 teaspoon salt
4 green onions, chopped
1 cup sliced fresh mushrooms
1 tablespoon butter
8 eggs
Freshly ground pepper to taste
8 ounces cream cheese, softened
2 cups evaporated milk
2 cups shredded Swiss cheese
1 cup shredded cooked chicken
2 tablespoons chopped fresh basil

Line a 10-inch pie plate with the pie pastry, trimming and fluting the edge. Bake at 350 degrees for 5 minutes or until partially browned; set aside.

Place the zucchini in a colander; sprinkle with salt. Drain for 20 to 30 minutes; squeeze out excess moisture.

Sauté the green onions and mushrooms in the butter in a small skillet.

Beat the eggs and pepper in a mixer bowl. Add the cream cheese and evaporated milk. Beat until smooth.

Sprinkle half of the Swiss cheese over the pie crust. Layer the chicken, mushrooms, green onions and zucchini over the Swiss cheese. Sprinkle with the remaining Swiss cheese.

Pour the egg mixture over the layers. Top with fresh basil.

Bake at 350 degrees for 1 hour. Cool for 15 minutes before serving.

Southwest Quiche

yields 8 servings

*If it's Friday or Saturday at The Dove's Nest, that usually means Quiche Day.
One of our customers' favorites is this combination of Southwest flavors.*

1/2 recipe Basic Pie Crust Dough (page 133)
2 cups shredded Monterey Jack cheese
3/4 cup chopped smoked turkey
1/2 cup chopped green chilies
1/2 cup corn
1/4 cup chopped red bell pepper
1/4 cup chopped red onion
1/4 cup minced fresh cilantro
8 eggs
1 teaspoon salt
1/2 teaspoon garlic powder
1 teaspoon ground cumin
1/2 teaspoon Tabasco sauce
1 1/2 to 2 cups evaporated milk

Line a 10-inch pie plate with the pie pastry, trimming and fluting the edge. Bake at 350 degrees for 5 minutes or until partially browned.

Layer half of the cheese, turkey, chiles, corn, bell pepper, onion, remaining cheese and cilantro in the partially baked crust.

Beat the eggs, salt, garlic powder, cumin and Tabasco sauce in a mixer bowl. Add the evaporated milk, beating well. Pour over the layers.

Bake at 350 degrees for 1 hour or until a knife inserted near the center comes out clean. Cool for 15 minutes before serving.

Southwest Strata

yields 12 servings

This is a great "do-ahead" entrée if you're planning for company. I often offer it as a daily special and our customers love it served with our Caesar Salad, found on page 69.

6 flour tortillas
2 (8-ounce) cans chopped green chiles, drained
8 ounces smoked turkey, thinly sliced
4 cups shredded Monterey Jack cheese
1 cup frozen corn, thawed
5 eggs
2 cups milk
Dash of Tabasco sauce
1/2 tablespoon garlic powder
Freshly ground pepper to taste
1/2 cup chopped fresh cilantro

Line a greased 9x13-inch baking pan with the tortillas.

Layer the chiles, turkey, cheese and corn 1/2 at a time in the prepared pan.

Beat the eggs, milk, Tabasco sauce, garlic powder and pepper in a bowl. Pour over the layers.

Top with the cilantro. Chill, covered, overnight.

Bake, uncovered, at 350 degrees for 50 to 60 minutes. Cool and cut into squares to serve.

Southwestern Crab Meat Soufflé

yields 12 servings

This is perfect for brunch, served with a fruit salad.

12 eggs
1 cup melted butter
2 cups cottage cheese, drained
16 ounces Monterey Jack cheese, shredded
1 (4-ounce) can chopped green chiles, drained
1 cup whole kernel corn
1 cup crab meat
1 cup flour
2 teaspoons baking powder
1 teaspoon curry powder
1 teaspoon garlic powder
Salt and pepper to taste
1/2 cup finely chopped fresh cilantro

Combine the eggs, butter, cottage cheese, Monterey Jack cheese, chiles and corn in a large bowl; mix well.

Stir in the crab meat, flour, baking powder, curry powder, garlic powder, salt and pepper.

Spoon into a buttered 9x13-inch baking pan. Sprinkle with the cilantro.

Bake at 350 degrees for 1 hour or until set. Cool slightly and cut into 12 portions to serve.

Grilled Mahimahi with Red Onion Couscous and Chunky Papaya-Avocado-Citrus Vinaigrette

yields 4 servings

For the vinaigrette

Juice of 6 limes
Juice of 3 oranges
3 cups vegetable oil
2 papayas, cubed
2 avocados, cubed
2 tablespoons sugar
1 teaspoon salt
1 bunch fresh cilantro, chopped

Combine the lime and orange juices in a bowl. Add the oil gradually, whisking constantly until combined.

Add the papayas, avocados, sugar, salt and cilantro, mixing well.

For the mahimahi

4 (8-ounce) mahimahi or swordfish fillets
Pinch of salt
1 tablespoon vegetable oil

Sprinkle the fillets with salt and brush with the oil.

Grill over hot coals for 5 minutes. Turn and grill for 2 minutes longer.

For the couscous

4 cups chopped red onions
2 tablespoons vegetable oil
1 cup red wine
1 tablespoon balsamic vinegar
4 cups chicken stock
2 (8-ounce) packages couscous
Salt and pepper to taste

Sauté the onions in the oil in a skillet over medium heat for 10 minutes. Add the wine and vinegar. Cook for 5 minutes to reduce, stirring occasionally. Add the chicken stock.

Bring to a boil; remove from heat. Stir in the couscous. Let stand, covered, for 10 minutes. Season with salt and pepper.

To assemble

Spoon a mound of the couscous in the center of each serving plate. Spoon the vinaigrette around the couscous. Place the mahimahi on top of the couscous.

Smoked Salmon and Goat Cheese Quiche

yields 10 servings

I love this sinfully rich quiche. We often make it as a lunch special, but it is also great when prepared as mini-quiches for hors d'oeuvre.

1/2 recipe Basic Pie Crust Dough (page 133)
1 1/2 cups grated Parmesan cheese
1/3 pound smoked salmon
3 green onions, chopped
8 eggs
8 ounces cream cheese, softened
2 ounces goat cheese
1 1/2 cups evaporated milk
1/2 teaspoon freshly ground pepper
2 tablespoons chopped fresh basil

Line a 10-inch pie plate with the pie pastry, trimming and fluting the edge. Bake at 350 degrees for 5 minutes or until partially baked.

Sprinkle with half the Parmesan cheese. Layer with the salmon and green onions.

Beat the eggs, cream cheese and goat cheese in a mixer bowl until smooth. Add the evaporated milk and pepper, beating well.

Pour over the layers. Sprinkle with the remaining Parmesan cheese and the basil.

Bake at 350 degrees for 1 hour or until a knife inserted in the center comes out clean. Cool for 15 minutes before serving.

Salmon with Chipotle Sesame Vinaigrette and Fried Basmati Rice with Shellfish

yields 4 servings

For the vinaigrette
1 chipotle or smoked jalapeño
1 cup toasted sesame seeds
1/3 cup fish sauce
2/3 cup rice vinegar
1 tablespoon chopped garlic
1 tablespoon grated ginger
1 tablespoon chopped lemon grass
1 bunch cilantro, chopped
1 tablespoon chopped fresh basil
1 tablespoon chopped fresh mint
Juice of 2 limes

Combine the pepper, sesame seeds, fish sauce, vinegar, garlic, ginger, lemon grass, cilantro, basil, mint and lime juice in a blender container.

Process until thoroughly mixed.

For the fried rice
2 tablespoons sesame oil
4 cups cooked Basmati rice
1 teaspoon chopped garlic
1 teaspoon grated ginger
1/3 cup soy sauce
2 tablespoons brown sugar
1 egg, lightly beaten
4 oysters, shucked
4 shrimp, peeled, deveined
4 scallops
4 crawfish
2 teaspoons fish sauce
2 tablespoons rice vinegar
1/2 cup sliced green onions

Heat the oil in a large skillet until it begins to smoke. Add the rice and sauté for 1 minute. Add the garlic, ginger, soy sauce and brown sugar. Sauté until the rice is dark brown, stirring frequently.

Cook the egg in a small nonstick skillet until set, forming a thin omelet. Slice into thin strips and add to the rice mixture. Add the oysters, shrimp, scallops, crawfish, fish sauce, vinegar and green onions.

Cook for 4 minutes or until the seafood is cooked through.

Salmon with Chipotle Sesame Vinaigrette and Fried Basmati Rice with Shellfish

continued

For the salmon
4 salmon fillets
Salt to taste
2 tablespoons sesame oil

Season the salmon with salt. Heat the sesame oil in a nonstick skillet over medium heat. Add the salmon. Cook for 4 minutes. Turn and cook for 2 minutes longer.

To assemble

Spoon a mound of the rice in the center of each serving plate and top with the salmon.

Drizzle the vinaigrette around the plate. Serve immediately.

Pecan-Crusted Rainbow Trout, Scalloped Sweet Potatoes and Smoked Tangerine Butter Sauce

yields 4 servings

For the sweet potatoes

4 sweet potatoes, very thinly sliced
1 1/2 cups whipping cream
1/4 cup packed brown sugar
1/4 teaspoon nutmeg
1/2 teaspoon cinnamon
Pinch of cayenne
1/2 teaspoon salt

✻ Layer the sweet potato slices in a greased 9x9-inch baking dish, packing closely.

✻ Combine the cream, brown sugar, nutmeg, cinnamon, cayenne and salt in a small bowl; mix well. Pour over the sweet potatoes.

✻ Bake, covered with foil, at 350 degrees for 50 minutes. Bake, uncovered, for 20 minutes longer.

For the trout

2 cups ground pecans
1/2 teaspoon salt
4 trout fillets
2 cups flour
6 eggs, beaten
1/2 cup butter
Juice of 1 lemon

✻ Mix the ground pecans and salt in a flat bowl. Dust the trout with flour, dip in the eggs and then coat with the pecan mixture.

✻ Melt the butter in a sauté pan over medium heat. Place the trout skin side up in the sauté pan. Cook for 2 to 3 minutes; turn. Cook for 30 seconds longer or until brown.

✻ Place on a serving plate and drizzle with the lemon juice.

Pecan-Crusted Rainbow Trout, Scalloped Sweet Potatoes and Smoked Tangerine Butter Sauce

continued

For the sauce

2 heads of garlic, cut into halves crosswise
2 large onions, cut into quarters
10 tangerines, cut into halves
1/2 cup maple syrup
1 quart freshly squeezed orange juice
1 cup whipping cream
2 cups butter, softened
Juice of 1 lemon

Cold smoke the garlic, onions and tangerines with pecan wood. (See page 141 for instructions on Smoking.) Sauté the garlic and onions in a large deep skillet for 5 to 10 minutes or until the onions are translucent. Add the maple syrup.

Sauté the mixture for 10 minutes longer or until brown. Add the orange juice. Squeeze the juice from the tangerines into the skillet and add the tangerine halves.

Simmer for 1 hour or until the mixture becomes syrupy, stirring occasionally. Strain into a 2-quart saucepan, squeezing solids to extract all liquid.

Heat the strained liquid until it begins to simmer. Add the cream.

Simmer gently until the mixture thickens; remove from heat.

Add the butter a little at a time, whisking constantly until blended. Stir in the lemon juice.

To assemble

Drizzle the sauce over the trout. Serve immediately with sweet potatoes.

Sourdough-Breaded Rainbow Trout with Buttermilk and Chive Whipped Potatoes and Smoked Crawfish Sauce

yields 4 servings

For the sauce

5 cloves of garlic
1/2 small onion
1 rib of celery
5 tomatoes
1 cup white wine
2 cups strong crawfish stock
1 (8-ounce) can tomato sauce
1 teaspoon chopped thyme
1 teaspoon chopped basil
1 teaspoon Creole seasoning
1/4 cup butter
Juice of 1 lemon
1 cup cooked crawfish
Salt to taste

Smoke the garlic, onion, celery and tomatoes. (See page 141 for instructions on Smoking.) Chop the vegetables finely.

Sauté in a medium saucepan over medium heat for 5 minutes. Add the wine, crawfish stock and tomato sauce.

Simmer for 5 minutes, stirring occasionally. Add the thyme, basil and Creole seasoning.

Simmer for 5 minutes, stirring occasionally. Cool slightly. Purée in a blender. Return to the saucepan.

Whip in the butter and lemon juice. Stir in the crawfish and salt.

For the potatoes

3 large potatoes, peeled and cubed
1/4 cup butter
1/2 cup (or more) buttermilk
1/4 cup finely chopped fresh chives

Boil the potatoes in water in a saucepan until tender; drain.

Beat with the butter in a mixer bowl until smooth. Add the buttermilk gradually, beating constantly until the potatoes are fluffy. Stir in the chives.

Sourdough-Breaded Rainbow Trout with Buttermilk and Chive Whipped Potatoes and Smoked Crawfish Sauce

continued

For the trout

1 small loaf sourdough bread, sliced
4 Rainbow trout fillets
1 teaspoon salt
1 cup flour
5 eggs, beaten
1/2 cup butter
Juice of 1 lemon

❧ Toast the bread slices. Process in a food processor until fine crumbs form. Pour into a shallow bowl.

❧ Season the trout with salt. Dust with the flour, dip in eggs and coat with the bread crumbs.

❧ Melt the butter in a sauté pan over medium heat. Add the trout skin side up. Sauté for 2 to 3 minutes. Turn and cook for 30 seconds longer. Drizzle with the lemon juice.

To assemble

❧ Spoon a mound of the potatoes in the center of each serving plate. Place the trout on top.

❧ Drizzle the sauce around the edge of the plate.

Seared Ahi Tuna with
Thai Salad and Fried Rice Noodles

yields 4 servings

*This is the dish we prepared live on "Good Morning Texas." It's a beautiful presentation
and very popular on our dinner menu in the spring.*

For the dressing
1/2 cup fish sauce
1/2 cup rice wine vinegar
1/4 cup soy sauce
1 tablespoon chopped garlic
1 tablespoon chopped lemon grass
1 tablespoon grated fresh ginger or pickled ginger
1 serrano, seeded, minced
Juice of 2 limes

❧ Combine the fish sauce, vinegar, soy sauce, garlic, lemon grass, ginger, pepper and lime juice in a medium bowl. Whisk until well mixed.

For the salad
2 small packages rice noodles
1 cup mixed fresh field greens
(radicchio, escarole, frisée)
1 cup shredded napa cabbage
1 red bell pepper, cut in julienne strips
1 cup snow peas, blanched
1 cup each bean sprouts, sliced cucumbers
and grated carrots
1/4 cup each chopped fresh basil, cilantro and mint

❧ Fry the rice noodles using package directions.

❧ Combine with the greens, cabbage, red pepper, peas, bean sprouts, cucumbers, carrots, basil, cilantro, mint and the dressing in a large salad bowl. Toss gently to coat.

For the tuna
1/4 cup sesame oil
1/4 cup vegetable oil
4 (8- to 10-ounce) Ahi tuna fillets

❧ Heat the sesame oil and vegetable oil in a large nonstick skillet over high heat. Add the tuna.

❧ Sear for 1 to 2 minutes on each side, leaving the center rare. Serve with the salad.

❧ For variety garnish with wabasi sauce, reduced-sodium soy sauce, toasted sesame seeds or toasted black sesame seeds.

Buttermilk, Wild Rice and Pecan Pancakes

yields 12 servings

*Andrew and I first had these pancakes on our honeymoon while snow skiing at Lake Louise, Canada.
This is our version. It's a wonderful side dish with wild game.*

3 cups water
2/3 cup wild rice
1 1/2 teaspoons salt
1/2 cup sifted flour
1/2 teaspoon baking powder
1/2 teaspoon baking soda
1/4 teaspoon pepper
1/2 cup buttermilk
1 large egg
1 tablespoon whipping cream
1/2 cup chopped toasted pecans
1 1/2 tablespoons finely chopped shallot
1 teaspoon (or more) olive oil

Combine the water, rice and 1 teaspoon of the salt in a medium saucepan. Bring to a boil; reduce heat.

Simmer for 40 minutes or until the rice is tender. Drain and cool to room temperature.

Mix the flour, baking powder, baking soda, pepper and remaining 1/2 teaspoon salt in a medium bowl. Whisk the buttermilk, egg and whipping cream in a small bowl. Add to the flour mixture, stirring to mix. Fold in the rice, pecans and shallot.

Heat the olive oil in a large nonstick skillet over medium heat. Drop the batter by tablespoonfuls into the skillet, spreading to form 3-inch circles.

Cook for 2 minutes on each side or until golden brown, adding more oil if necessary.

May prepare the rice a day ahead and store, covered, in the refrigerator.

Wild Mushroom and Three-Cheese Lasagna

yields 8 servings

For the sauce

1 (1-ounce) package dried porcini mushrooms
1 cup hot water
3 tablespoons olive oil
1 medium onion, chopped
12 ounces button mushrooms, sliced
6 to 8 ounces fresh shiitake mushrooms, stemmed, sliced
4 large cloves of garlic, minced
1 tablespoon chopped fresh rosemary, or 2 teaspoons
dried rosemary
1/8 teaspoon dried crushed red pepper
1/2 cup dry red wine
1 (28-ounce) can crushed tomatoes with purée
Salt and pepper to taste

Rinse the porcini mushrooms in cold water. Place in a small bowl with the hot water. Soak for 30 minutes to soften. Remove from water, squeezing excess liquid back into the bowl; reserve the liquid. Chop the porcini mushrooms, discarding any hard stems.

Heat the olive oil in a large heavy saucepan. Sauté the onion for 8 minutes or until tender. Add the porcini, button and shiitake mushrooms and the garlic.

Sauté for 5 minutes or until the mushrooms are tender. Add rosemary and red pepper.

Sauté for 30 seconds. Add the wine and strain in the reserved mushroom liquid.

Bring to a boil. Cook for 5 minutes or until the liquid is reduced by half. Add the tomatoes. Reduce the heat to medium-low.

Simmer for 15 minutes or until the sauce is thickened, stirring occasionally. Season with salt and pepper.

Wild Mushroom and Three-Cheese Lasagna

continued

For the lasagna

2 (15-ounce) containers ricotta cheese
1/2 cup freshly grated Parmesan cheese
1/3 cup prepared pesto sauce
Salt and pepper to taste
2 eggs, beaten
1 egg yolk
12 (about) lasagna noodles
20 ounces Montrachet or other soft mild
goat cheese, crumbled
1 tomato, seeded, chopped
Fresh basil or rosemary

Combine the ricotta cheese, Parmesan cheese and pesto in a medium bowl. Season with salt and pepper. Add the eggs and egg yolk, beating well. May be prepared ahead and stored, covered, in the refrigerator.

Cook the noodles using package directions. Drain and rinse in cold water.

Spread 1/4 of the sauce in a 9x13-inch baking dish. Layer half the noodles, half the ricotta cheese mixture, 1/4 of the remaining sauce and 1/3 of the goat cheese in the prepared dish. Top with the remaining noodles, pressing to compact the layers. Layer with the remaining ricotta cheese mixture, remaining sauce and remaining goat cheese, pressing to compact the layers. May be prepared ahead and stored, covered, in the refrigerator. Let stand at room temperature for 1 hour before baking.

Cover with foil and place on a baking sheet. Bake at 350 degrees for 35 minutes. Bake, uncovered, for 35 minutes longer or until the cheese melts and bubbles.

Top with the chopped tomato. Let stand for 15 minutes. Garnish with basil or rosemary.

Portobello Mushrooms, Scallops and Goat Cheese Manicotti with Red Pepper Coulis

yields 4 servings

For the manicotti

8 manicotti shells
1/4 cup olive oil
2 tablespoons chopped garlic
5 portobello mushrooms, coarsely chopped
1 pound Calico Bay scallops
1/2 cup white wine
8 ounces ricotta cheese
8 ounces goat cheese
1 egg, beaten
1 tablespoon chopped fresh basil
Salt and pepper to taste

Cook the manicotti shells using package directions until al dente. Drain and cool slightly.

Heat the olive oil in a large skillet. Sauté the garlic, mushrooms and scallops over high heat for 2 to 3 minutes. Add the wine.

Cook until the wine evaporates, stirring frequently. Remove from heat and let stand to cool slightly.

Mix the ricotta cheese, goat cheese, egg and basil in a small bowl. Stir in the scallop mixture. Season with salt and pepper.

Spoon the mixture into a pastry bag with no tip. Pipe into the manicotti shells. Arrange in a baking dish.

Bake, covered with foil, at 350 degrees for 10 minutes or until heated through.

For the coulis

8 red bell peppers, seeded, coarsely chopped
2 tablespoons sugar
Salt and pepper to taste

Place the peppers in a 2-quart saucepan. Fill with water to cover.

Bring to a boil over high heat. Remove from heat and drain.

Process in a blender until puréed.

Combine with the sugar in a 2-quart saucepan. Simmer for 5 minutes. Season with salt and pepper.

To assemble

Arrange the manicotti shells on a warmed serving plate. Top with the warm coulis.

Onion Tart
yields 8 servings

There is nothing better in the spring when onions are sweet. We use Texas 1015 onions.
You may substitute one pint of half-and-half for the milk and whipping cream.

1/2 recipe Basic Pie Crust Dough (page 133)
16 ounces Swiss cheese, shredded
2 tablespoons flour
2 large onions, thinly sliced
4 eggs
1 cup whipping cream
1 cup milk
1/2 teaspoon curry powder
1/4 teaspoon ground nutmeg
2 drops of Tabasco sauce
1 teaspoon salt
Freshly ground pepper to taste

Line a 10-inch pie plate with the pie pastry, trimming and fluting the edge.

Toss the Swiss cheese with flour in a small bowl. Spread evenly over the pie pastry. Separate the onion slices into rings. Arrange over the cheese mixture.

Beat the eggs with the cream, milk, curry powder, nutmeg, Tabasco sauce, salt and pepper. Pour over the cheese and onions.

Bake at 350 degrees for 45 minutes. Serve warm.

Nutted Wild Rice

yields 8 to 10 servings

My dear friend, Britton Wilson, gave me this recipe years ago and I have prepared it for my own dinner parties and large catered events. It's always a popular side dish and a great accompaniment for game and meat dishes.

1 cup wild rice
$4^2/_3$ cups chicken stock
7 tablespoons butter
1 cup brown rice
4 shallots, minced
4 ounces mushrooms, cut into quarters
Salt and pepper to taste
1 cup pecan halves
$^1/_2$ cup chopped fresh parsley

Combine the wild rice with 2 cups of the chicken stock and 2 tablespoons of the butter in a saucepan. Cook, covered, for 1 hour or until all liquid is absorbed and the rice is tender.

Combine the brown rice, the remaining $2^2/_3$ cups chicken stock and 2 tablespoons of the butter in another saucepan. Bring to a boil; reduce heat to low. Cook for 50 minutes or until the liquid is absorbed.

Melt the remaining 3 tablespoons of the butter in a skillet over medium heat. Add the shallots and mushrooms. Sauté for 5 minutes.

Toss the wild rice, brown rice, shallots and mushrooms in a large bowl. Season with salt and pepper. Add the pecans and parsley, mixing well.

Southwestern Squash Casserole

yields 8 servings

*An old roommate of mine, Kay Kelly Rains, sent me this recipe several years ago
and it has been a family favorite ever since.*

8 medium yellow squash, sliced
1/2 cup sour cream
3 tablespoons butter
1 cup shredded Cheddar cheese
1/2 teaspoon salt
2 eggs, beaten
2 tablespoons chopped chives
6 slices bacon, crisp-fried, crumbled
1 (4-ounce) can chopped green chiles, drained
1/4 cup chopped fresh cilantro
12 saltine crackers, crumbled
Paprika to taste

Place the squash in a saucepan with water to cover. Cook over high heat until tender; drain well.

Combine with the sour cream, butter, cheese, salt, eggs, chives, bacon, green chiles, cilantro and crackers in a bowl, mixing well.

Spread evenly in a buttered baking dish. Sprinkle with paprika.

Bake at 350 degrees for 30 minutes or until browned.

Vegetable Casserole with Goat Cheese and Herbs

yields 4 servings

When you want a lighter dinner, it is hard to beat this dish. Serve with a loaf of French bread and a bottle of red wine. Andrew and I enjoy this at home after a long day in the restaurant.

2 tablespoons olive oil
1 medium onion, cut into $1/2$-inch slices
1 medium red bell pepper, cut into $1/2$-inch strips
$1/4$ cup finely chopped garlic
$1/2$ eggplant, peeled, thinly sliced
5 Roma tomatoes, thinly sliced
2 large zucchini, thinly sliced
Salt and pepper to taste
3 tablespoons chopped fresh herbs (thyme, oregano and basil)
2 tablespoons olive oil
8 ounces Montrachet or other soft mild goat cheese

Heat 2 tablespoons olive oil in a large heavy skillet over medium heat. Add the onion and red bell pepper. Sauté for 5 minutes or until tender. Add the garlic. Sauté for 1 minute longer.

Spread the mixture evenly in a 9x13-inch baking dish. Arrange the eggplant slices evenly over the mixture. Layer with alternating lengthwise rows of tomatoes and zucchini, overlapping slightly. Season with salt and pepper.

Sprinkle with the herbs. Drizzle with the remaining 2 tablespoons olive oil. Season with salt and pepper. Crumble the goat cheese over the top.

Bake at 350 degrees for 50 minutes or until the vegetables are very tender and lightly browned, basting with the pan juices occasionally.

SWEET ENDINGS

©'96 Marilyn Goss

Sweet Endings

Apricot Cheesecake

yields 10 to 12 servings

Use gingersnap crumbs with this cheesecake for a delicious complement to the apricots.

For the crust

1 1/2 cups gingersnap crumbs
3 tablespoons melted butter

Mix the gingersnap crumbs with the melted butter in a bowl. Pat over the bottom and up side of a 9-inch springform pan.

For the filling

1 cup dried apricots
Grated zest of 1 orange
24 ounces cream cheese, softened
3/4 cup sugar
4 eggs
1/2 cup sour cream

Place the apricots in a saucepan with water to cover. Simmer for 20 minutes to soften; drain.

Purée the apricots with the orange zest in a food processor.

Beat the cream cheese in a mixer bowl until light and fluffy. Add the sugar, beating at low speed until smooth. Add the eggs 1 at a time, beating well after each addition.

Fold in the sour cream and the apricot purée. Spoon into the prepared crust.

Bake at 325 degrees for 50 to 60 minutes or until set. Cool on a wire rack. Chill for 8 hours or longer before serving.

Espresso Hazelnut Cheesecake

yields 14 servings

For the crust

1 (8-ounce) package butter biscuit cookies
1/2 cup husked hazelnuts, toasted
2 tablespoons sugar
1 teaspoon ground cinnamon
5 tablespoons melted unsalted butter

Butter the bottom and side of a 2¾-inch high 9-inch springform pan. Wrap the outside of the pan with a double layer of foil.

Process the cookies, hazelnuts, sugar and cinnamon in a food processor until finely ground. Add the butter.

Process until moist clumps form. Press the mixture onto the bottom and up side of the prepared pan. Chill while preparing the filling.

For the filling

32 ounces cream cheese, softened
1¼ cups sugar
4 large eggs
1 cup sour cream
1/2 cup plus 2/3 cup chilled whipping cream
3 tablespoons instant espresso powder
2 tablespoons warm water
2 teaspoons vanilla extract
3/4 cup husked hazelnuts, toasted, coarsely chopped
Chocolate-covered espresso beans

Beat the cream cheese in a mixer bowl until light and fluffy. Add the sugar, beating until smooth. Add the eggs 1 at a time, beating well after each addition. Beat in the sour cream and 1/2 cup of the whipping cream.

Dissolve the espresso powder in the warm water in a bowl. Add to the creamed mixture with the vanilla, beating well. Stir in the hazelnuts.

Spoon into the prepared pan. Place the pan in a large baking pan filled with enough water to come halfway up the side of the springform pan.

Bake at 350 degrees for 1¼ hours or until puffed and almost set. Turn off the oven. Let the cheesecake stand in the oven with the door ajar for 1 hour.

Remove from the pan of water and cool on a wire rack. Chill, covered with foil, for 8 to 10 hours before serving. Loosen the cheesecake by running a knife around the side of the pan before removing.

Beat the remaining 2/3 cup whipping cream in a mixer bowl until stiff peaks form. Spoon into a pastry bag fitted with a large star tip. Pipe around the top edge of the cheesecake. Garnish with chocolate-covered espresso beans.

Cherry Pineapple Pecan Cobbler

yields 12 servings

I almost didn't include this recipe because it is so simple. It is the only dessert we prepare at lunch for which we use a mix. We tried to take it off the menu, but our customers begged to have it back.

1 (8-ounce) can crushed pineapple
$^1/_2$ cup sugar
1 (21-ounce) can cherry pie filling
1 (2-layer) package butter cake mix
$^1/_2$ cup melted butter
1 cup chopped pecans

Spread the undrained pineapple in the bottom of a buttered 9x13-inch baking pan. Sprinkle with the sugar. Cover with the cherry pie filling.

Sprinkle the cake mix evenly over the cherries. Drizzle with the melted butter. Sprinkle with the pecans.

Bake at 350 degrees for 1 hour.

Serve warm with vanilla ice cream.

Cold Amaretto Soufflé

yields 6 servings

24 (about) whole or 12 split ladyfingers
1 envelope unflavored gelatin
1/2 cup cold water
3/4 cup amaretto
6 egg yolks, at room temperature
3/4 cup sugar
6 egg whites, at room temperature
1 tablespoon fresh lemon juice
1 cup whipping cream
Toasted slivered almonds

Cut a strip of waxed paper 8 inches wide and 2 inches longer than the circumference of a 7-inch soufflé dish. Fold the paper in half lengthwise and generously butter 1 side. Wrap the paper around the top of the soufflé dish, extending 2 1/2 inches above the rim. Staple or pin the overlapping edges. Tie a string around the dish to secure the collar. Stand the ladyfingers upright around the dish with sides touching. Trim one end flat if necessary.

Soften the gelatin in cold water in a small heatproof bowl for 5 minutes. Place the bowl in a pan of simmering water. Stir until the gelatin is completely dissolved. Remove from heat.

Stir in the amaretto. Let stand until cool. Chill for 30 minutes or until slightly thickened, stirring occasionally.

Beat the egg yolks in a large mixer bowl until pale yellow in color. Add 1/4 cup of the sugar gradually, beating until the mixture is thickened. Add the gelatin mixture, beating until light and fluffy.

Beat the egg whites in a mixer bowl until soft peaks form. Add the remaining 1/2 cup sugar gradually, beating well. Add the lemon juice, beating until the egg whites are stiff but not dry. Fold into the egg yolk mixture.

Whip the cream in a small mixer bowl until soft peaks form. Fold into the egg yolk mixture.

Spoon the mixture gently into the prepared dish, smoothing the top. Chill for 3 hours or until firm. May chill for up to 2 days. Serve garnished with almonds.

Hot Brownie Soufflé with Vanilla Ice Cream Sauce
yields 4 servings

For the soufflé
Sugar to taste
1/2 cup butter, cut into small pieces
4 ounces unsweetened chocolate, coarsely chopped
1 tablespoon instant coffee powder
1 tablespoon rum or orange liqueur
1 cup sugar
4 egg yolks, beaten, at room temperature
1 teaspoon vanilla extract
1/4 cup flour
5 egg whites, at room temperature

Butter a 1-quart soufflé dish and sprinkle with sugar.

Melt the butter and chocolate in a large heavy saucepan over very low heat, stirring until smooth. Dissolve the coffee powder in the rum. Add to the chocolate mixture with 1/2 cup of the sugar, egg yolks and vanilla, mixing well. Stir in the flour. May prepare several hours ahead to this point and set aside, but reheat before proceeding.

Beat the egg whites in a large mixer bowl until soft peaks form. Add the remaining 1/2 cup sugar gradually, beating constantly until egg whites are stiff but not dry.

Fold 1/4 of the egg whites into the chocolate. Fold the chocolate mixture into the remaining egg whites very gently. Spoon the batter into the prepared dish. Sprinkle with sugar.

Place the soufflé dish on the center oven rack. Bake at 450 degrees for 5 minutes. Reduce the oven temperature to 400 degrees. Bake for 20 minutes longer or until puffed. Serve immediately with the sauce.

For the sauce
1 pint rich vanilla ice cream
2 tablespoons rum or orange liqueur

Soften the ice cream in a bowl for 10 minutes at room temperature or for 30 minutes in the refrigerator.

Add the rum, beating until smooth. Pour into a small bowl and serve immediately with the soufflé.

Coffee Walnut Toffee

yields 2 pounds

1¹/4 cups unsalted butter
1 cup sugar
¹/3 cup packed golden brown sugar
¹/3 cup water
1 tablespoon dark unsulfured molasses
2 teaspoons instant espresso powder
¹/2 teaspoon ground cinnamon
¹/4 teaspoon salt
2 cups coarsely chopped toasted walnuts
4¹/2 ounces imported white chocolate, finely chopped
4¹/2 ounces imported bittersweet (not unsweetened) chocolate, finely chopped

Melt the butter in a heavy 2¹/2-quart saucepan over low heat. Add the sugar, brown sugar, water, molasses, espresso powder, cinnamon and salt. Cook until the sugars are dissolved completely, stirring constantly with a wooden spatula.

Cook over medium heat for 20 minutes or until a candy thermometer registers 290 degrees. Stir slowly but constantly, scraping the bottom of the pan. Remove from heat.

Fold in 1¹/2 cups of the walnuts. Pour the mixture onto a small buttered baking sheet, tilting the baking sheet to spread the toffee to a ¹/4-inch thickness.

Sprinkle the white and bittersweet chocolates alternately over the toffee. Let stand for 1 minute. Spread the chocolates with the back of a spoon, tilting the baking sheet to form an even layer. Swirl the chocolates with the tip of a knife to create a marbleized pattern. Sprinkle with the remaining ¹/2 cup walnuts.

Chill for 1 hour or until firm. Break into pieces.

Store in an airtight container in the refrigerator for up to 2 weeks. Serve cold or at room temperature.

The Dove's Nest Carrot Cake

yields 12 servings

This is my favorite recipe for carrot cake because it has crushed pineapple in it that keeps it so good and moist.

For the cake

2 cups flour
2 teaspoons baking powder
1$\frac{1}{2}$ teaspoons baking soda
1 teaspoon salt
2 teaspoons cinnamon
2 cups sugar
1$\frac{1}{2}$ cups vegetable oil
4 eggs, beaten
2 cups grated carrots
1 (8-ounce) can crushed pineapple, drained
$\frac{1}{2}$ cup chopped pecans

Sift the flour, baking powder, baking soda, salt and cinnamon into a large bowl. Add the sugar, oil and eggs, mixing well. Stir in the carrots, pineapple and pecans. Pour into 3 greased and floured 9-inch cake pans.

Bake at 350 degrees for 30 to 35 minutes or until the layers test done.

For the frosting

$\frac{3}{4}$ cup butter, softened
12 ounces cream cheese, softened
1$\frac{1}{2}$ teaspoons vanilla extract
1$\frac{1}{2}$ (1-pound) packages confectioners' sugar
1$\frac{1}{2}$ cups chopped pecans
Zest of 1 orange

Cream the butter, cream cheese and vanilla in a mixer bowl until light and fluffy. Add the confectioners' sugar gradually, beating well after each addition. Stir in the pecans and orange zest. May add a small amount of orange juice to achieve desired spreading consistency.

To assemble

Spread the frosting between each layer and over the top and side of the cake.

Chocolate Truffle Cake with Rum Cream

yields 10 to 12 servings

*My mother-in-law, Carolyn Burch, made this delicious dessert for a Sunday night dinner and
I was so impressed I prepare it quite often now in the restaurant.*

For the cake

1/2 cup unsalted butter, softened
7 ounces semisweet chocolate, crumbled
1 tablespoon Grand Marnier
1 tablespoon rum
1 teaspoon vanilla extract
1 tablespoon flour
5 egg yolks, at room temperature
3/4 cup sugar
5 egg whites, at room temperature
2 tablespoons confectioners' sugar
Orange zest

Butter and flour a 10-inch springform pan with 1 tablespoon of the butter. Line the pan with waxed paper.

Melt the chocolate and the remaining butter over low heat in a heavy nonstick saucepan. Pour into a bowl. Stir in the Grand Marnier, rum, vanilla and flour.

Beat the egg yolks with half of the sugar in a mixer bowl until pale yellow. Stir into the chocolate mixture.

Beat the egg whites in a mixer bowl until soft peaks form. Add the remaining sugar gradually, beating until stiff peaks form. Fold into the chocolate mixture. Pour the mixture into the prepared pan.

Bake at 275 degrees for 1 hour and 20 minutes. Cool on a wire rack. Remove side of pan.

For the rum cream

1 pint whipping cream
1 tablespoon Grand Marnier
1 tablespoon rum
1 teaspoon vanilla extract
3/4 cup sugar

Beat the cream in a mixer bowl until soft peaks form. Add the Grand Marnier, rum and vanilla, beating constantly. Add the sugar gradually, beating until stiff peaks form.

To assemble

Slice the cake. Dust with the confectioners' sugar.

Spoon a dollop of the rum cream on each serving. Garnish with orange zest.

Fudge Brownie Pudding Cake

yields 10 to 12 servings

This rich and wonderful cake separates into layers as it bakes, making its own sauce.

1 cup flour
2/3 cup unsweetened baking cocoa
3/4 teaspoon double-acting baking powder
1/4 teaspoon salt
2 eggs
1 cup sugar
6 tablespoons melted unsalted butter
1/4 cup milk
1 teaspoon vanilla extract
1/4 cup chopped walnuts
3/4 cup packed light brown sugar
1 1/3 cups boiling water

Combine the flour, 1/3 cup of the cocoa, baking powder and salt in a medium bowl.

Whisk the eggs, sugar, butter, milk and vanilla in a large bowl. Add the flour mixture, stirring until mixed. Fold in the walnuts.

Spread the batter evenly in an ungreased 8-inch square cake pan.

Whisk the remaining 1/3 cup cocoa, brown sugar and boiling water in a bowl. Pour over the batter.

Place on the middle oven rack. Bake at 350 degrees for 35 to 40 minutes. Cake will not appear set when first removed from the oven, but do not overbake.

Serve warm with coffee ice cream.

Coconut Cream Cake

yields 12 servings

This recipe appeared in The Dallas Times Herald in 1987 and I've had it in my files ever since. It's a great recipe for summer weather because it's served cold. We make it at The Dove's Nest and serve it with fresh strawberries.

1 (2-layer) package pudding-recipe white cake mix
3 eggs, beaten
1/3 cup vegetable oil
1 cup water
1/2 teaspoon coconut extract
1 cup canned cream of coconut syrup
1 (14-ounce) can sweetened condensed milk
1 cup whipping cream
1 tablespoon sugar
1 cup flaked coconut
Fresh strawberries

Combine the cake mix, eggs, oil and water in a bowl, mixing well. Stir in the coconut extract. Pour into a greased and floured 9x13-inch cake pan.

Bake at 350 degrees for 30 minutes or until the cake tests done.

Mix the coconut syrup and condensed milk in a small bowl. Pour over the hot cake.

Let stand until cool.

Beat the whipping cream with the sugar in a mixer bowl until soft peaks form. Spread over the cake.

Top with the flaked coconut. Serve with fresh strawberries.

Gingerbread with Pear Brandy Sauce

yields 8 servings

For the gingerbread

1 1/2 cups flour
1 teaspoon baking soda
1/2 teaspoon salt
1/2 teaspoon ground allspice
1/4 teaspoon ground cloves
1/4 teaspoon freshly grated nutmeg
1/2 cup unsalted butter, softened
1/2 cup packed dark brown sugar
2 eggs, at room temperature
1/4 cup dark unsulfured molasses
1 tablespoon grated fresh ginger
2/3 cup buttermilk
Confectioners' sugar

Butter and flour an 8-inch square cake pan.

Sift the flour, baking soda, salt, allspice, cloves and nutmeg into a medium bowl.

Cream the butter and brown sugar in a mixer bowl until light and fluffy. Add the eggs 1 at a time, beating well after each addition. Stir in the molasses and ginger. Stir in half of the dry ingredients and the buttermilk. Add the remaining dry ingredients, stirring until combined. Pour into the prepared pan and smooth the top.

Bake at 325 degrees for 40 minutes or until a wooden pick inserted in the center comes out clean. Cool slightly in the pan on a wire rack. Cut into squares. Dust with confectioners' sugar.

For the sauce

Peel from 1 lemon, cut into strips
2 cups water
1/2 cup sugar
1/4 cup fresh lemon juice
4 Bartlett pears, peeled, cut into quarters
1/4 cup poire Williams (clear pear brandy),
Cognac or brandy

Place the lemon strips in a large heavy nonreactive saucepan. Add the water, sugar and lemon juice.

Cook over medium heat until the sugar dissolves, stirring frequently. Add the pears.

Cook for 20 minutes or until tender. Transfer the pears to a bowl with a slotted spoon, reserving the liquid.

Simmer the reserved liquid until reduced to 3/4 cup. Discard half of the lemon strips. Remove the remaining lemon strips to a food processor container. Add the pears and the liquid. Process until smooth.

Strain through a sieve, pressing with the back of a spoon. Stir in the poire Williams. Serve over the warm gingerbread. May prepare ahead and refrigerate. Bring to room temperature before serving.

Strawberry Cake

yields 12 servings

*When spring arrives and fresh strawberries are in abundance, our customers
start asking for this delightfully moist cake.*

For the cake

1 (3-ounce) package strawberry gelatin
1/2 cup cold water
1 (2-layer) package white cake mix
4 eggs
1 cup vegetable oil
3 tablespoons flour
1/2 (10-ounce) package frozen strawberries, thawed

Dissolve the gelatin in cold water. Combine with the cake mix, eggs, vegetable oil, flour and strawberries in a mixer bowl. Beat for 5 minutes. Pour into 3 greased and floured round cake pans.

Bake at 325 degrees for 30 to 35 minutes or until the layers test done. Cool in the pans on wire racks.

May substitute fresh strawberries for the frozen strawberries.

For the frosting

6 tablespoons butter, softened
2 cups confectioners' sugar
1/2 (10-ounce) package frozen strawberries, thawed

Cream the butter, confectioners' sugar and strawberries in a mixer bowl until light and fluffy, adding additional confectioners' sugar if needed for desired consistency.

May substitute fresh strawberries for the frozen strawberries.

To assemble

Spread the frosting between the layers and over the top and side of the cake.

Almond Apricot Biscotti

yields 40 servings

2³/4 cups sifted flour
1¹/2 cups sugar
¹/2 cup chilled unsalted butter, cut into pieces
2¹/2 teaspoons baking powder
1 teaspoon salt
1 teaspoon ground ginger
3¹/2 ounces imported white chocolate, cut into pieces
1²/3 cups whole almonds, toasted
2 large eggs
¹/4 cup plus 1 tablespoon apricot-flavored brandy
2 teaspoons almond extract
1 (6-ounce) package dried apricots, chopped

Combine the flour, sugar, butter, baking powder, salt and ginger in a food processor container. Process until a fine meal forms. Add the white chocolate. Process until finely chopped. Add the almonds. Pulse 6 to 8 times to chop coarsely.

Beat the eggs, brandy and almond extract in a large bowl. Add the flour mixture and apricots, stirring until moistened.

Line a 12x18-inch cookie sheet with foil. Butter and flour the foil. Shape the dough into three 12-inch long by 2-inch wide strips and place on the prepared cookie sheet, leaving a space between each strip. Chill for 30 minutes or until the dough is firm.

Place the cookie sheet on the center oven rack. Bake at 350 degrees for 30 minutes or until golden brown. Cool completely on the cookie sheet on a wire rack.

Remove the logs to a work surface. Cut into ³/4-inch wide slices with a sharp knife. Place half of the cookies cut side down on the cookie sheet.

Reduce the oven temperature to 300 degrees. Bake for 10 minutes. Turn and bake for 10 minutes longer. Cool completely on a wire rack. Repeat the process with the remaining cookies. Store in airtight containers for up to 2 weeks.

Caramel Brownies

yields 15 servings

So easy and so decadent!

2 (14-ounce) packages caramels
1 1/3 cups evaporated milk
2 (2-layer) packages German chocolate cake mix
2 cups butter, softened
2 cups chopped nuts
2 cups semisweet chocolate chips

Place caramels and 2/3 cup of the evaporated milk in a heavy saucepan. Cook over low heat until caramels are melted, stirring frequently.

Combine the cake mix, the remaining 2/3 cup evaporated milk and butter in a mixer bowl. Beat until moistened. Stir in the nuts. Spoon half of the batter into a nonstick 9x13-inch baking pan.

Bake at 350 degrees for 6 to 10 minutes.

Sprinkle chocolate chips over the top. Spread the caramel mixture over the chocolate chips. Cover with the remaining batter.

Bake for 17 to 20 minutes or until the edges pull from the sides of the pan.

Let stand until cool. Chill for 20 minutes before cutting into squares.

Kahlúa Fudge Brownies

yields 15 servings

*These dense and decadent brownies are truly a chocolate lover's dream,
and always a favorite with our customers.*

4 ounces unsweetened chocolate
1 cup butter
1½ tablespoons instant espresso powder
2 cups sugar
4 eggs
1 cup flour
¼ teaspoon salt
1 teaspoon vanilla extract
1 tablespoon Kahlúa or other coffee-flavored liqueur
2 cups chopped nuts
1 cup semisweet chocolate chips

Melt the chocolate with the butter in a heavy saucepan over low heat, stirring constantly; remove from heat. Add the espresso powder, stirring until dissolved.

Stir in the sugar. Add the eggs 1 at a time, beating well after each addition. Add the flour, salt, vanilla and Kahlúa, mixing well.

Fold in the nuts and chocolate chips. Spread in a greased and floured 9x13-inch baking pan.

Bake at 350 degrees for 30 minutes or until the center is set. Cut into squares to serve.

Chocolate Chip Cookies

yields 8 dozen

Everybody has a favorite chocolate chip cookie recipe and this one is mine. I learned from my mother-in-law, Carolyn Burch, that a little cinnamon is a great secret ingredient.

5 cups rolled oats
4 cups flour
2 teaspoons baking powder
2 teaspoons baking soda
1 teaspoon salt
2 cups butter, softened
2 cups sugar
2 cups packed brown sugar
4 eggs
2 teaspoons vanilla extract
1 teaspoon ground cinnamon
4 1/2 cups semisweet chocolate chips
3 cups chopped nuts

Process the oats in a blender until finely ground. Combine with the flour, baking powder, baking soda and salt in a large bowl; mix well.

Cream the butter, sugar, brown sugar, eggs and vanilla in a mixer bowl until light and fluffy. Add the flour mixture, stirring until moistened. Stir in the cinnamon, chocolate chips and nuts.

Shape the dough into golf-sized balls. Arrange on an ungreased cookie sheet.

Bake at 350 degrees for 20 to 30 minutes or until golden brown.

Remove to a wire rack to cool completely.

Oatmeal Cookies
yields 8 dozen

*When I was growing up, we had a neighbor in Dallas named Dorothy Strozier. Every time someone
new moved onto our street, Dorothy would bake a batch of these delicious cookies for them. For years she refused
to share the recipe, but after the Stroziers moved away, she sent a copy of the recipe to my mom and apologized
for being so selfish with a recipe that had brought so much happiness. My mom has continued
her tradition in their neighborhood, where everyone calls these "Tiny Cookies" after my dad, whose
nickname is Tiny because he is such a large man.*

2 cups shortening
2 cups sugar
2 cups packed brown sugar
4 eggs
1/4 cup vanilla extract*
1/4 cup ground cinnamon*
4 cups flour
2 teaspoons baking soda
2 teaspoons salt
4 cups rolled oats

Cream the shortening, sugar, brown sugar, eggs, vanilla and cinnamon in a mixer bowl until light and fluffy.

Combine the flour, baking soda, salt and oats in a bowl. Stir into the creamed mixture.

Shape the dough into golf-sized balls. Place on a greased cookie sheet.

Bake at 350 degrees for 30 minutes. Cool on wire racks.

*Trust me, these measurements are correct. You will love the results.

Old-Fashioned Tea Cakes

yields 6 dozen

My grandmother, "Nanny," made these for my mom as she was growing up in Alabama and, in turn, my mom has baked them for me. Some of my favorite memories are of coming home from school and having a plate of freshly baked tea cakes waiting for me.

1 cup shortening
2 cups sugar
2 eggs
1 teaspoon baking powder
1 teaspoon baking soda
1/2 cup buttermilk
1 teaspoon salt
1 teaspoon vanilla extract
4 cups flour

Cream the shortening, sugar and eggs in a mixer bowl until light and fluffy. Stir in the baking powder.

Dissolve the baking soda in the buttermilk. Stir into the creamed mixture. Add the salt and vanilla. Stir in the flour gradually until a soft dough forms.

Drop by spoonfuls onto a greased cookie sheet. Press with a damp cloth wrapped around the bottom of a glass.

Bake at 350 degrees for 10 to 15 minutes or until golden brown. Cool on wire racks.

Buttermilk Pie

yields 8 servings

A true southern favorite. A customer asked me one day, "What is Buttermilk Pie?" I replied,
"You're obviously not from the South." He said, "Well, does South New York, count?"

$^1/_2$ recipe Basic Pie Crust Dough (page 133)
$^1/_4$ cup flour
$^1/_2$ cup melted butter
$^1/_2$ cup buttermilk
$1^1/_2$ cups sugar
$^1/_2$ teaspoon vanilla extract
3 eggs

Line a 9-inch pie plate with the pie pastry, trimming and fluting the edge.

Combine the flour, butter, buttermilk, sugar, vanilla and eggs in a mixer bowl. Beat until smooth.

Pour into the prepared pie plate.

Bake at 350 degrees for 1 hour.

Chocolate Bourbon Pecan Pie

yields 8 servings

*Our most popular dessert at The Dove's Nest. How can you go wrong with three
of the best ingredients around . . . chocolate, bourbon, and pecans?*

1/2 recipe Basic Pie Crust Dough (page 133)
3/4 cup sugar
1/2 cup melted butter, cooled
1/2 cup flour
2 eggs
1 cup semisweet chocolate chips
1 cup pecans
3 tablespoons bourbon

Line a 9-inch pie plate with the pie pastry, trimming and fluting the edge.

Bake at 350 degrees for 5 minutes or until very lightly browned.

Combine the sugar, butter, flour and eggs in a mixer bowl, beating well. Stir in the chocolate chips, pecans and bourbon. Pour into the prepared pie shell.

Bake at 350 degrees for 30 to 35 minutes or until set.

Cool slightly before slicing. Serve with vanilla ice cream.

Peanut Butter and Banana Pie

yields 12 servings

How I remember Sunday afternoons! After having eaten ourselves silly, my mom would start playing the old gospel hymns on the piano while Uncle Roy sang along. After a while we would all gather around for Aunt Effie's Peanut Butter Pie. At The Dove's Nest we add a layer of bananas and a little praline liqueur—but don't tell Aunt Effie!

For the crust

2¹/2 cups graham cracker crumbs
¹/2 cup melted unsalted butter
¹/4 cup salted ground peanuts

✣ Combine the graham cracker crumbs, butter and peanuts in a bowl, mixing well.

✣ Press over the bottom and side of a 10-inch pie plate.

For the filling

8 ounces cream cheese, softened
3 cups confectioners' sugar
2 cups chunky peanut butter
12 ounces whipped topping
2 tablespoons vanilla extract
1 tablespoon praline liqueur (optional)
1 large banana, sliced

✣ Beat the cream cheese in a mixer bowl until light and fluffy. Add the confectioners' sugar gradually, beating until smooth. Beat in the peanut butter and whipped topping. Stir in the vanilla and praline liqueur. Spoon half of the mixture into the prepared pie plate. Top with the sliced banana. Cover with the remaining mixture.

✣ Freeze for 1 hour before serving. Serve with your favorite chocolate sauce and whipped cream.

Pecan Butterscotch Pie

yields 8 servings

2 1/2 cups pecan halves
1/4 cup sugar
1 cup packed light brown sugar
1/4 cup cornstarch
1/4 teaspoon salt
2 1/2 cups milk
4 egg yolks
6 tablespoons unsalted butter
1 1/2 teaspoons vanilla extract
1 egg white
1 cup whipping cream
1 tablespoon dark rum

Chop the pecans coarsely in a food processor. Remove 1/2 cup of the pecans and spread on a baking sheet. Toast for 6 to 8 minutes or until lightly browned. Let stand until cool. Add the sugar to the remaining pecans. Process until finely ground; set aside.

Sift the brown sugar, cornstarch and salt into a large saucepan. Whisk 1/2 cup of the milk with the egg yolks in a medium bowl. Add the remaining milk and whisk briskly. Pour into the saucepan with the brown sugar mixture, stirring until blended.

Cook over medium-high heat for 7 to 8 minutes or until the mixture thickens, whisking constantly. Remove from heat. Add the butter and vanilla, stirring until the butter is melted. Stir in the toasted pecans. Place a sheet of waxed paper directly on the surface of the mixture and set aside.

Add the egg white to the ground pecans in the food processor container. Process for 4 seconds or until completely mixed. Spread the pecan mixture over the bottom and partially up the side of a 9-inch pie plate sprayed with nonstick cooking spray.

Bake at 350 degrees for 10 minutes. Cool on a wire rack for 30 minutes.

Pour the custard mixture into the prepared pie plate. Cool for 2 hours or until room temperature. Chill, covered, for 3 hours.

Beat the whipping cream in a mixer bowl until soft peaks form. Add the rum, beating until stiff peaks form. Spread over the pie and serve.

Basic Pie Crust Dough

yields two 9-inch pie shells

3 cups flour
3 tablespoons sugar
1 teaspoon salt
1 cup chilled unsalted butter, cut into pieces
2 egg yolks, lightly beaten
1/4 cup ice water

Combine the flour, sugar and salt in a medium bowl. Cut in the butter with a pastry blender or knife until the mixture is crumbly. Add the egg yolks and enough water 1 tablespoon at a time until the dough begins to hold together.

Shape into a large ball; divide into halves. Flatten each half into a disk. Wrap in plastic wrap and chill for 30 minutes.

May be made ahead and stored in the refrigerator for 1 day.

Roll the chilled dough into a circle 2 inches larger than the pie plate and 1/8 inch thick on a lightly floured surface. Trim the edges and finish as desired.

The Dove's Nest Caramel Sauce

yields 3 cups

2 cups packed light brown sugar
1 cup butter
1 cup light corn syrup
$1/4$ cup whipping cream
1 teaspoon vanilla extract
$1/4$ teaspoon salt
1 teaspoon praline liqueur (optional)

Combine the brown sugar and $1/2$ cup of the butter in a heavy saucepan. Bring to a boil.

Add the corn syrup, cream, vanilla, salt and praline liqueur, whisking briskly. Reduce heat to low.

Simmer for 3 minutes, stirring constantly. Remove from heat and whisk in the remaining $1/2$ cup butter until smooth.

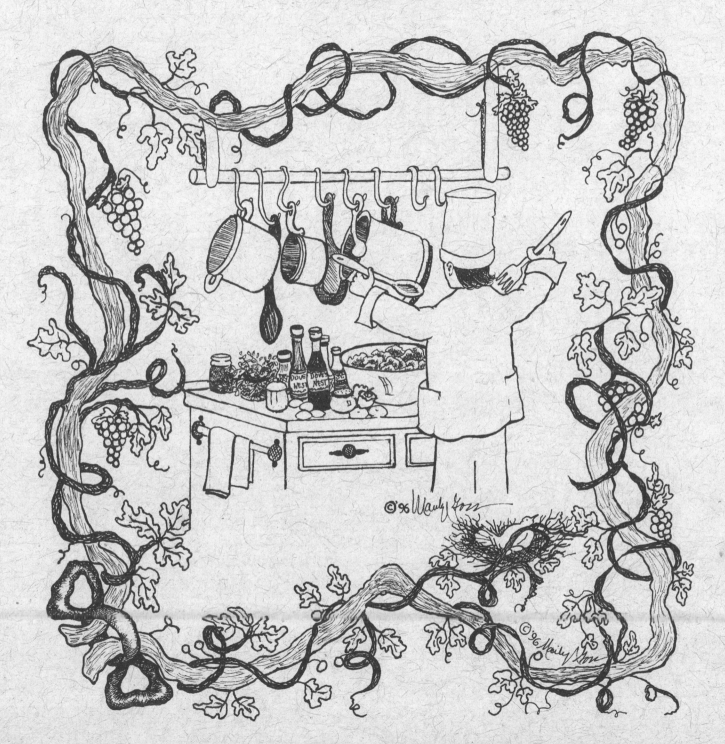

Basic Chicken Stock and Demi-Glace

yields 4 cups chicken stock or 2 cups demi-glace

1/2 large onion, unpeeled
3 cloves of garlic, unpeeled
1 chicken carcass
1 cup chopped carrot
1 cup chopped celery
3 to 4 sprigs fresh thyme, or 1/2 teaspoon dried thyme
1 bay leaf
1/2 tablespoon peppercorns
5 to 6 cups water

Place the onion, garlic, chicken carcass, carrot, celery, thyme, bay leaf and peppercorns in a large stockpot. Add enough water to cover.

Bring to a boil; reduce heat. Simmer for 2 hours, adding additional water if necessary. Simmer for 20 minutes after each addition of water. For a richer flavor, cook until the stock is reduced by half.

Remove from heat. Let stand until cool. Skim off the fat and strain.

May store the stock for 3 to 4 days in the refrigerator or up to 2 months in the freezer.

To prepare a demi-glace, add 1 1/2 tablespoons cornstarch mixed with 1 1/2 tablespoons cold water to the stock. Simmer until the stock is reduced to 2 cups and is thick enough to coat a spoon.

Brown Veal Stock and Demi-Glace

yields 2 quarts stock or 1 quart demi-glace

6 pounds veal bones
1 large onion, cut into halves
1/2 head of garlic
1 cup each chopped turnips, carrots and celery
6 to 8 sprigs fresh thyme, or 1 teaspoon dried thyme
6 bay leaves
1 cup chopped parsley
1/2 teaspoon peppercorns
6 large tomatoes, chopped
1 (6-ounce) can tomato paste
2 quarts red wine
1 1/2 gallons water or chicken stock

Place the veal bones in a roasting pan. Bake at 450 degrees for 1 1/2 hours.

Add the onion, garlic, turnips, carrots and celery. Bake for 30 minutes longer or until the bones are browned.

Remove from the oven and transfer the bones and vegetables to a large stockpot. Add the thyme, bay leaves, parsley, peppercorns, tomatoes and tomato paste.

Place the roasting pan over high heat; add the wine. Cook for 2 minutes, stirring to deglaze the pan. Pour into the stockpot. Add enough water to cover. Bring to a boil; reduce heat to medium-low. Simmer for 6 hours, stirring occasionally.

Reduce heat to low. Simmer for 4 hours longer, adding additional water or stock as needed. Simmer for 1 hour after adding water.

Remove from heat. Let stand until cool. Skim off the fat and strain the stock into another pan.

Store for 1 week in the refrigerator or up to 2 months in the freezer.

To prepare a demi-glace, add 1 1/2 tablespoons corn-starch mixed with 1 1/2 tablespoons cold water to the stock. Simmer until the stock is reduced by half and is thick enough to coat a spoon.

Grainy Mustard Demi-Glace

yields variable servings

1/2 cup prepared whole grain mustard
1 cup veal demi-glace (page 137)
1 tablespoon balsamic vinegar
Salt and pepper to taste

Combine the mustard, demi-glace, vinegar, salt and pepper in a saucepan; mix well.

Simmer until reduced to the desired consistency, stirring occasionally.

Roasted Red Pepper Demi-Glace

yields variable servings

2 roasted red bell peppers, peeled, seeded (page 140)
1 cup veal demi-glace (page 137)
1/2 teaspoon minced jalapeño
Salt and pepper to taste

Purée the bell peppers, demi-glace, jalapeño, salt and pepper in a blender.

Strain into a saucepan. Simmer until reduced to the desired consistency, stirring occasionally.

Oven-Dried Tomatoes

15 Roma tomatoes, cut lengthwise into halves
10 cloves of garlic, minced
1 cup olive oil
1 tablespoon freshly ground pepper
1 tablespoon salt

Combine the tomatoes, garlic, olive oil, pepper and salt in a bowl, tossing to coat. Spread on a baking pan.

Bake at 200 degrees for 12 to 18 hours.

Flavoring Oils

To infuse herbs in oil, first use an olive oil (but not an extra-virgin olive oil) and purée a full cup of fresh herbs with a small amount of the olive oil. Filter the olive oil and add additional olive oil until you achieve the desired flavor.

To infuse spices, heat the spice and olive oil together slowly—less than 1 minute. Filter the olive oil and add additional olive oil if the flavor is too strong.

To infuse roasted garlic, roast a head of garlic seasoned with salt and pepper in $1/4$ cup olive oil at 350 degrees for 30 minutes or until soft and caramelized. Drain off the olive oil, and reserve the roasted garlic for another use.

Roasted Garlic

yields 4 servings

Baked heads of garlic are wonderful served in soups, vegetables, and alongside roasted meats.
It's also delicious squeezed out of the skin and spread on a slice of crusty French bread.

4 whole heads of garlic
2 tablespoons olive oil
1/4 cup Basic Chicken Stock (page 136), or canned broth
1/2 teaspoon dried thyme
1/4 teaspoon dried rosemary
1/2 teaspoon freshly ground pepper
1/4 teaspoon coarse salt

Cut the tips from each head of garlic. Place in a small baking dish. Drizzle with the olive oil and chicken stock. Sprinkle with the thyme, rosemary, pepper and salt.

Bake, covered with foil, for 30 to 45 minutes, basting frequently. Remove foil. Bake for 10 to 15 minutes longer or until the garlic is tender.

Roasted Peppers

Preheat the broiler. Place the whole peppers on a baking tray. Place on the top rack of the oven. Roast until the skin becomes puffed and charred, turning as needed to blacken the entire surface.

Place the peppers in a sealable plastic bag and seal tightly. Let stand for several minutes to steam. Remove the peppers and strip off the charred skin. Remove the stems and seeds. Chop or purée as needed.

Smoke Cooking

≈ We use primarily pecan wood at The Dove's Nest and recommend using a large amount of wood charcoal so that the coals will burn slowly. (Charcoal briquets, especially those infused with liquid starter, can give off fumes that will ruin the flavor of the food you are smoking.)

≈ The rule of thumb to follow when smoking is to allow 30 minutes smoking time per pound of meat, fish, or game.

≈ Wood chips or branches are soaked in water and placed on top of the wood charcoal once it has burned down to a gray ash. If the wood is still green, you do not need to soak it first. Dry pieces, however, must be soaked well so they will give off smoke instead of burning. If the wood chips burn down, keep adding fresh chips so the smoke will stay constant.

≈ The easiest smokers to use at home are the outdoor cookers sold as "smokers" at most grocery or hardware stores. The pan that holds the coals is in the bottom of the 2- to 3-foot tall cooker. A pan to hold water rests between the coals and the cooking rack; this will help keep your meat from drying out. A dome lid traps the smoke.

Smoke Flavoring (Cold Smoking)

≈ This process does not cook the meat or vegetables—it flavors them. A small Weber Kettle Grill can be used for this. These small dome-covered cookers are designed primarily for grilling steaks on a small patio, but their convenient size and design makes them ideal for smoking in small quantities.

≈ Light 4 to 5 pieces of wood charcoal. Mound the hot coals in the bottom of the cooker and let them burn down to a gray ash. Spread out in a single layer and place soaked or green wood pieces over the ashes.

≈ This process lowers the heat of the coals to "cold smoke." Do not place the meat or vegetables directly over the coals. Instead, place them around the outer edges or on a piece of foil. Allow approximately 20 minutes to cold smoke.

≈ Gas grills can also be used by setting the temperature on low, and then turning off the heat. Place smoked wood on the preheated grill rocks. Place your meat or vegetables on the cool side of the grill or on the top upper rack. Close the lid and smoke about 20 minutes.

Index